Lover of my Soul

ALAN D. WRIGHT

LOVER
of my
SOUL

DELIGHTING IN GOD'S
PASSIONATE LOVE

Multnomah Publishers *Sisters, Oregon*

LOVER OF MY SOUL
published by Multnomah Publishers, Inc.

© 1998 by Alan D. Wright
International Standard Book Number: 1–57673–269–X

Cover photograph by Masao Mukai/Photonica
Designed by Kirk DouPonce
Printed in the United States of America

For information:
MULTNOMAH PUBLISHERS, INC.•POST OFFICE BOX 1720•SISTERS, OREGON 97759

Library of Congress Cataloging-in-Publication Data:
Wright, Alan D.
Lover of my soul/Alan D. Wright.
   ISBN 1-57673-269-X (alk. paper)   p. cm.
  1. God—Love. I. Title.
BT140.W75 1998   98-18707
242—dc21   CIP

01 02 03 04 05 — 10 9 8 7 6 5 4 3 2

_____ *For Mom* _____

Did you know that...

> *while your tears splashed into God's palms, you were teaching my heart to be tender?*

> *while your silly bursts of laughter made God grin, you were teaching me to look for joy?*

> *while the aroma of your intercession was inhaled by God, He was breathing out the blessing upon me?*

As your deep love has delighted me, may you delight afresh in God's deep love for you.

Acknowledgments

Thanks to:

Anne, my wife, friend, lover…Others marvel at your glow, slap their sides at your stories, and warm in your presence. But I spy your soft, secret soul, and my heart still flutters.

Bennett…I love you past the moon, around the sun, over the big oak tree, down the sliding board, and back through your bedroom window and…more than that.

My families—the Wrights, Wrens, Lynches, Curries, Budds…You've been so supportive of my writing. I think the publisher could break a profit off your purchases alone.

Richard Moore…I'd been courted by God and had said my vows, but when you prayed for me, God took me into His bridal chamber and gave me passion and joy.

Linda Cooke, my secretary…I'm amazed. I've brought nothing but more work into your life, and you've brought nothing but more smiles into mine.

My partners in ministry on staff with me…You're the dream team.

Reynolda Presbyterian Church…You're a preacher's dream come true.

Dan Benson, my editor…for seeing beauty in the Savior and wanting beauty in books. Every conversation with you brings fresh dew to my heart and fresh ink to my pen.

My Multnomah partners…You make it all so fun. Thanks for letting me write.

CONTENTS

MEET THE LOVER OF YOUR SOUL

"You will call me 'my husband.'"
Hosea 2:16

I want a lover.

Don't gasp. I don't mean the made-for-TV version of a lover. I mean *lover* in its simplest definition: "one who loves." I just want someone to love me. Don't you?

I'll admit it. I want someone to hold me, cuddle me, kiss me. I want someone who would climb mountains just to be with me. I want someone who smiles just at the thought of me. I want someone who believes in me. I want someone who absolutely adores me. Give me a lover and I'll be happy.

You might say that a lover shouldn't be a Christian's chief desire. You might say I should hunger for nobler things like eternal purpose, God's will, or personal holiness. I understand your protest.

For years I found it almost embarrassing to confess my longing for love—like admitting a glaring weakness in my life, a gaping flaw in my character. But why apologize for a simple hunger? Hunger was God's idea. Adam and Eve had to eat even before the Fall. It's a good thing our bellies crave food, or we'd all die from malnutrition. It's a good thing our souls hunger for love, or we'd never seek the intimacy we need. Unfortunately we don't often feed our growling tummies wisely. Junk food stops the growl but contaminates the body. Likewise, lust and superficial relationships stop the heart's growl momentarily but contaminate the yearning soul.

I'm not alone in looking for love. The silly antics people undergo in the name of romance prove how desperately we search for love. The psychic hotlines are getting rich from people who want to know if love is in their future. Romance novels sell by the mega-thousands. A TV soap-opera character can lose one husband to death, another to divorce, and a third via a mysterious disappearance in six short months. But instead of throwing up their hands in disbelief and turning off the tube, viewers tune in the next day in hopes that a new love is on its way for their favorite character.

If you think yourself immune to the hunger for love, reflect for a moment with me. Didn't our hunger for affection start before we were even born?

I don't remember all the details, but I imagine it was the only reason I decided to come out into the world. The womb was cozy and safe. The voices outside my insulated home sounded loving. But I craved to see the faces that went with the voices. The hands that patted my uterine home seemed affectionate, but I wanted to be embraced by those hands. So as soon as I emerged, I cried until someone held me snugly and spoke to me tenderly.

Think about it. As babies, we weren't the least bit bashful about our longings for love. We soaked up every ounce of affection we could get.

Over time, my hunger for love changed but never diminished. As a toddler, if I scraped my knee, it was second nature to ask for a kiss on the sore place. As a kid, I wanted a best buddy who would build forts with me and stick up for me when I needed him. As a teenager, I wanted a girl to smile at me in homeroom, dance with me at the prom, and kiss me good night on her front porch.

*M*y desire for affection didn't die after adolescence. Soon I wanted a wife. I met mine in a Bible study. What a wonderful interweaving of womanly beauty! Pretty but unpretentious. Winsome but wise. Playful but mysterious.

It was invigorating to be so attracted to her. But my soul really soared when I discovered she was likewise drawn to me. I remember the night we first talked. It wasn't even a date—just conversation under the brightly lit Carolina sky. While we spoke, my heart thumped and my mind danced. Time slipped away. We talked all night, and I went straight to my 8 A.M. class. I have no recollection of the class—in fact, no recollection of the course! Who could care? I was falling in love. The world stood still, and duty seemed to disappear.

The love grew. One day that woman said she'd love me forever, and she slipped a ring on my finger. When she put her head on the pillow next to mine, the candlelight flickered, and love came even closer.

Was that the fulfillment of my love desire? Had my hunger been satisfied once and for all? By no means.

Once married, I continued to relish her affection. And now, twelve years later—who could have imagined it?—I spend a lot of time hounding my three-year-old Bennett for hugs, butterfly kisses, and "nose mashes."

I'm not ashamed of it. In fact, I'm thankful for my lifelong hunger for love. Without it I wouldn't have looked for true Love. Without my yearning, I never would have found eternal Affection. Without it, I never would have met the Lover of my soul.

Can you admit that you want a lover too? Good. I've penned these thoughts for you. Maybe you long for love because you've tasted how delicious a little affection can be—and now you're hungering for the main course. Or maybe life's not given you much of a love appetizer—and like a citizen of a famined land, you're just looking for a morsel of food.

Either way, there's good news in the pages to come. It's good news because, if you're unmarried, you don't have to find a mate to feel loved. If you're in a painful marriage, you don't have to get out of it to find affection. No matter what your circumstances are, if you yearn for passion, you're about to be swept off your feet. If you hunger for love, pull up a chair to the banquet table. You're invited to a feast.

I want to tell you about Someone who would climb mountains just to be with you. In fact, He climbed a mount called Calvary. I want to tell you about Someone who smiles at just the thought of you. In fact, He makes His face to shine upon you. I want to tell you about Someone who utterly adores you. In fact, He wants to hold your hand forever.

I want to introduce you to your Lover.

A romantic tale awaits. It is the greatest love story in history.

It has all the familiar characters: a heroic prince, a vulnerable maiden, a seductive tempter. Its plot has all the ingredients: a hero wooing his beloved and winning her hand, a maiden wandering from purity, and a moving climax of two walking together in forever love.

You might be surprised where you'll find this love story. It's all in the Bible. But it's not the story of Adam and Eve, Jacob and Rachel, or Samson and Delilah. It's the story of the God who loved His people so much that He called them His bride. It's the story of a heavenly Prince who so desired His beloved's hand in marriage that He gave up all to win her. It's a story of how the eternal Groom still woos the bride in order to welcome her into eternity with Him.

The Scriptures spill over with this image of marriage. A quick sampling to whet your appetite:

"...as a bridegroom rejoices over his bride, so will your God rejoice over you." (Isaiah 62:5)

"'In that day,' declares the LORD, 'you will call me "my husband"; you will no longer call me "my master."'" (Hosea 2:16)

"'For your Maker is your husband—the LORD Almighty is his name.... The Lord will call you back as if you were a wife deserted and distressed in spirit—a wife who married young, only to be rejected,' says your God." (Isaiah 54:5–6)

"'...a man will leave his father and mother and be united to his wife....' This is a profound mystery—but I am talking about Christ and the church." (Ephesians 5:31–32)

"I saw the Holy City, the new Jerusalem, coming down out of heaven from God, prepared as a bride beautifully dressed for her husband." (Revelation 21:2)

My Christian mentors have always taught me not to overemphasize feelings in my walk with God. "Feelings come and go," I was rightly instructed. "It doesn't matter if you feel loved; just accept the truth of the Bible." They were mostly correct. Whether I *feel* saved doesn't determine my eternal destiny. Whether I *feel* loved by God doesn't alter the enduring promises of His Word.

We don't go on feelings, but it sure is good to feel what we're going on. It's astonishing to watch men and women feel the affectionate embrace of the Lord for the first time. It's as though they awaken to a new dawn. Like a bride, they take on a strange, new glow. Worship becomes a wonder. Prayer, a privilege. Servanthood, a fragrant sacrifice.

I can no longer settle for the saying, "Feelings don't matter; just trust the Word." Instead, I fervently pray with Paul that all "may have power...to grasp how wide and long and high and deep is the love of Christ" (Ephesians 3:18). God's love is not a concept to be intellectualized by the mind. It is a reality to be embraced by the heart. To long for the touch of His affection is not a sign of flimsy faith. It's an authentic hunger for what our souls need most.

Maybe the reason we've not felt God's affection more is that we've been too bashful to call Jesus the Lover of our souls. We've worshiped God as the Creator who owns the cosmos. We've proclaimed Him the King who rules the world. We've called on Him as the Father who cares for His children. But we've been too coy about the Groom who rejoices over His bride.

That's why I can hardly wait to tell you this love story.

Before we start, please note: This book will differ from ordinary romance books. You, beloved reader, are not a spectator in this tale. You are not going to experience someone else's passion vicariously. You are a leading character. So expect these pages to get personal. Marriage is, by definition, personal. And expect honesty. Relationships require truth—even if it digs deep. Get ready for your role in the romantic plot. Laugh some, cry some, dance some. But whatever you do, don't just listen to the story.

Now—the Groom is smiling. His heart is pounding with joyous anticipation as He watches His bride approach the threshold of the aisle. It's the moment He's wanted more than anything. Once He slides the ring on her finger, He won't ever take it back. Once the vows are spoken, He'll hardly be able to wait to whisk His bride away in His arms.

Remember, you are not in the audience watching this wedding. You are the bride. This is your celebration. You've never looked more beautiful than this moment. *Shh*—listen. The processional music has started. Go ahead; take the first step. All of heaven is standing to watch. The Love of your life awaits you at the altar. Take another step. It's time to say "I do." It's time to lift the veil. It's time to let the Lord be the Lover of your soul.

WOOED

CHAPTER ONE

WOOED

Oh LORD, you have enticed me, and I was enticed.
Jeremiah 20:7, NRSV

*P*reaching was in the man's bones. But hardly anyone wanted to sit through his sermons. He had a few supporters and a faithful office administrator. That was about it.

He thought about quitting a million times, but he couldn't. It wasn't that he needed the job. He had no family to support. No mortgage payments to make. Besides, he surely could have made a better living doing something else.

Maybe it takes a preacher to understand one; I know how he felt. He just *had* to preach. There's no other way to describe it.

But hardly a week went by that he didn't ask, like most preachers do at some point, "Why am I doing this? Why can't I have a normal life?"

Then one week things got really bad. The preacher was falsely accused of misconduct by some denominational officials, who proceeded to drag his name through the mud.

Amid the scandal the faithful preacher saw an image that put words to his feelings. He pictured himself as the wife of a noble-but-unpopular husband. Like the wife, he was bound to the Lord, his Husband. Divorce was out of the question. But to stay by the Lord's side meant he, like the wife, would receive the scorn meant for the Husband. As the preacher considered the image and pondered his predicament, he asked himself, "How did I wind up wed to God?"

He considered the incredible, compelling draw that God had upon his life. Then a shocking thought shot through his mind. His agony was great enough that he dared utter it aloud to God: "Lord, You seduced me!"

*B*efore you shake your head in disgust at the desperate preacher's choice of words, be clear about his meaning. The preacher didn't need Freudian therapy for some sexual hang-up. He just knew the depth of his love for the Holy God of Israel. The preacher had no other way to explain his irreversible connection to the Lord. He had no other terms to describe his irresistible attraction to the Word of God. He had no other image to explain a calling so strong that he could not let it go. So the preacher admitted it aloud. He had been allured by an altogether winsome God. He had been wooed by the heavenly Suitor's attractive promises. He had been smitten by the magnificence of Jehovah.

The preacher's name was Jeremiah. He really said it. "Lord, You seduced me!" He really meant it.

The New Revised Standard Version uses a more tasteful word: "O LORD, you have *enticed* me, and I was *enticed*" (Jeremiah 20:7, emphasis added). Other translations soften it even further. But the Hebrew word literally means "seduced." It's the same word used in the law that describes a man who lures a virgin to his bed (Exodus 22:16). It's the word the Philistine rulers used to tell

Delilah what they wanted her to do to Samson (Judges 16:5). But most compelling of all, God Himself used the word to describe how He planned to bring Israel out of exile: "Therefore I am now going to *allure* her; I will lead her into the desert and speak tenderly to her" (Hosea 2:14, emphasis added).

What does a man do to catch the attention of a lady? He might fill her home with flowers or perhaps send a single rose every day. He might serenade her, compose poetry for her, or write love notes to her on the Internet. In true courtship there is no room for pride. The suitor must pour out his heart.

But a wise suitor does not reveal all his qualities at once. He wants to attract his beloved, not smother her. He wants to intrigue her, not suffocate her. After all, a gentleman doesn't want to consume his sweetheart; he wants to commune with her. Most of all, he wants her to want *him*.

That's God's nature too. He could easily smother you, suffocate you, and consume you. He could easily engulf you, ensnare you, and enslave you. But the Lord doesn't need you as His possession. He already owns you. The heart of God longs for your freely given love. He wants you more as a willing bride than an unwilling slave. As He said: "You will call me 'my husband'; you will no longer call me 'my master'" (Hosea 2:16).

And so the Lord reveals His beauty to you little by little. He grants little samples of His grace so you will "taste and see that the LORD is good" (Psalm 34:8). He wants what every good husband wants in a bride—that she be comfortably content in His love yet genuinely desirous of deeper intimacy.

Maybe that's why Jesus taught so cryptically. He regularly tossed out puzzling statements like "You must be born again" (John 3:7).

He deliberately shocked people with His symbolism: "Destroy this temple, and I will raise it again in three days" (John 2:19).

The Messiah loved to whet His followers' appetites with mysterious allusions to coming attractions: "You believe because I told you I saw you under the fig tree. You shall see greater things than that" (John 1:50). He sometimes withheld information just for the purpose of intrigue. For example, when the first disciples asked Jesus where He was staying, the Nazarene replied simply, "Come...and you will see" (John 1:39).

Jesus was a fisherman casting lures, not a hunter spearing His prey. He was a shepherd leading His sheep, not a thief snatching lambs. And so He came not to scare us into submission but to woo us into fellowship.

*P*erhaps you have been walking hand in hand with this eternal Prince for many years. Maybe you have just begun your honeymoon. Or maybe you know this Messiah only by name. I don't know how much of His affection you have felt. But I know this for sure: You are where you are only because He wooed you.

You certainly didn't entice *Him*. Call me old-fashioned, but the perfect gentleman always goes first. *He* opens the door for her. *He* proposes to her. *He* says his vow first. *He* carries her across the threshold.

Jesus spelled it out: "No one can come to me unless the Father who sent me draws him" (John 6:44). And John made it equally plain: "This is love: not that we loved God, but that he loved us and sent his Son as an atoning sacrifice for our sins" (1 John 4:10).

I used to think the Bible was telling me, "Obey God. Yield to Him. Give your life to Him, then He will really love you." But that's not how a groom courts his bride. Here's the marvel of the gospel: God loves you. Always has, always will. Tenderly, passionately, the Groom is wooing you. Your hand in marriage is His highest desire. Your love, His greatest goal. Therefore, because He loves you so dearly, obey Him. Yield to Him. Give your life to the One who loves you most.

Imagine it. The King of the universe, who could smite you with a word or turn you into smoke with a single burst of light, takes time to entice you. Instead of consuming you, the Messiah decided to court you.

*W*hen a man's in love, he gets creative in his courtship. Check out how Steven got Lisa to say "I do."

Lisa is a dolphin fanatic. She stocks dolphin stuff on her living-room shelves and hangs dolphin pictures on her walls. So Steven, the sly guy, snatched Lisa by surprise one day and fulfilled her fantasy. He had arranged for the two of them to go behind the scenes at Sea World and swim with the dolphins.

The couple donned wet suits and dipped into the dolphin tank. Lisa got to touch the lovable bottlenoses, hold their fins, and swim with them. The trainer led the clever animals in a few neat tricks. Making Lisa's dream come true was a fine piece of courtship. But the real surprise came with the finale.

One of the dolphins bounced a giant beachball off its nose. As the ball sailed toward Lisa, she saw big letters spelling out: "Will you marry me?"[1]

*P*roposing in a dolphin tank was pretty clever. But where the heavenly Bridegroom proposed to us was unthinkable. He gave up a King's castle for a cave. He gave up bowing angels for baying animals. He gave up celestial aroma for barnyard stench. He came to swim in our puny tank and to let us swim with Him.

Steven's proposal just doesn't compare. Maybe if he'd become a dolphin. No, that doesn't compare either. Dolphins are gentle, lovable animals. Jesus "came to that which was his own, but his own did not receive him" (John 1:11). He not only let us touch Him—He let us tear Him. He not only let us stroke Him—He let us strike Him.

He was a Suitor courting His bride. He intended to spare no expense for her hand. He would pour out His heart, His heavenly riches. He would pour out His blood.

I'm not suggesting that theologians add *seductive* to the list of divine attributes in the Westminster Confession. Nor do I think you ought to use this word when you share the Bible's plan of salvation with others. Our world has become far too perverted to redeem such a suggestive word.

But I'm convinced you'll not know how much God loves you until you behold the extravagant way He courted you. You'll not feel His affection until you see His attractiveness. You'll not know the grandeur of God's grace until you know that He wooed you in order to win you.

CHAPTER TWO

PURSUED

Where can I flee from your presence?
Psalm 139:7

atricia loved to dance. As a young woman growing up in the Big Band era, she spent her Saturday nights waltzing, two-stepping, and jitterbugging at the local ballroom. One evening a man she'd never met asked her onto the dance floor. He was a pleasant man but a pitiful dancer.

The band played all kinds of great songs, but the man knew only one dance. "We danced the fox-trot, and then came a jitterbug rhythm, and he still would use the same old steps," Patricia says. After taking a break for a soft drink, the man compelled her onto the dance floor again. *Here we go again,* Patricia thought. *The same old two-step.*

Exasperated, Patricia tried to escape the clumsy dancer by excusing herself to the ladies' lounge. After hiding there a long time, she figured the oaf would have found another partner. Not so. When she came out of seclusion, there he was. "Like glue to wallpaper," she remembers. Patricia couldn't shed him. She bumbled around the dance floor with him the rest of the evening.

After the last dance, the persistent two-stepper asked to take Patricia home. When she emphatically declined, he asked for her phone number. Desperate to get away, she gave in and gave him her number. She figured it would be easier to say no over the phone anyway.

The following Sunday, Patricia was waiting by the curb to catch the bus. Imagine her dismay when the ballroom bumbler pulled up in a shiny new car, opened the door, and asked her to hop in. As Patricia was saying "No, thank you," the city bus pulled up behind his car.

The bus driver leaned on the horn, but the man refused to move his car. Embarrassed, Patricia finally jumped into the automobile. When she pointed to her friend's house where she wanted to be let out, the man didn't even slow down. Panicking, Patricia fumbled for the door handle and screamed, "Let me out!" Oddly enough, when he saw her dismay, the two-stepper slowed, made a calm U-turn, and stopped at Patricia's destination.

He wasn't odd just on the dance floor or in the car. He was also strange on the phone. Sometimes there would be a long, weird silence before he spoke. Often the diligent bachelor would phone and say, "Pat, I want to go to the movies." No matter how loudly Pat would say no, thirty minutes later he would show up at her door, smiling.

What was wrong with the man? Why couldn't he take no for an answer? Didn't he have any respect for Patricia's desires? Perhaps a better question is how could this man persist in the face of such rejection? How many noes could he take before giving up? Two months of this strange, persistent courtship elapsed before the bachelor explained.

When he did, it finally all made sense.

The man was totally deaf.

The well-educated bachelor was a proficient lip reader who had learned to use his voice remarkably well. He had learned to stumble around a dance floor without hearing music. He had learned to speak on the phone without ever hearing the other party's answer. He had learned to drive without hearing others' road rage.

He was a persistent suitor because he never heard the word no.

With a changed heart, Patricia patiently taught her new boyfriend a few new dance steps. After another six months, he offered her a diamond, and she accepted. Pretty amazing, huh? Patricia has been happily married for forty-three years to the man who turned a deaf ear to all her rejections.[1]

I know of only one suitor more persistent than Patricia's husband, and He persists not out of deafness but out of incredible, unconditional love.

*T*he longer I'm wed to Jesus Christ, the less credit I take for this spiritual marriage. As I examine the events of my life, I see that God has done much more than politely invite me into a relationship with Him—He has pursued me relentlessly. Every time I've tried to hide from Him, He's found me. Every time I've hurt myself by stumbling in my own sin, God has seized the moment to show me comfort. He told me He loved me in a thousand different ways before I ever told Him how much I love Him.

Can you see the incredible patience and perseverance God has shown for you? Consider your own life. Recall the events, people, and circumstances that have brought you to God. You may not even be able to explain what drew you to Him. Maybe you're not even sure why you're reading this book. But I know why. God is after you. Everywhere you go, God is there first.

> *Where can I go from your Spirit?*
>> *Where can I flee from your presence?*
> *If I go up to the heavens, you are there;*
>> *if I make my bed in the depths, you are there.*
> *If I rise on the wings of the dawn,*
>> *if I settle on the far side of the sea,*
> *even there your hand will guide me,*
>> *your right hand will hold me fast.*
>
> (Psalm 139:7–10)

onah experienced God's persistence when he tried to flee from the Lord. God told Jonah to go east to Nineveh; the prophet headed west to Spain. Tarshish was the farthest imaginable spot from Nineveh. It was as if God said, "Go to Alaska," and Jonah booked a cruise in the Caribbean. He wanted to lose God. But God never gets lost. The rebellious preacher couldn't sail faster or farther than God's pursuing love.

When a big storm arose at sea, the pagan sailors discovered Jonah's disobedience. Desperate, they decided to help Jonah fulfill his death wish and heaved the prophet overboard.

y little boy likes to playact Bible stories. His favorite game is David with his sling; Joshua with his horn finishes a distant second. But one day, two-year-old Bennett wanted to play

Jonah. He crawled up on the couch and announced, "This is the boat where I'm sleeping. There's a big storm. Daddy, you be the sailor who wakes me up."

Dutifully I rustled Jonah from his nap. "Wake up, wake up! There's a big storm," I cried.

"Well, just throw me into the water," my little Jonah prompted. So with a gentle toss, I removed Bennett from the couch—er, the boat—onto the carpet—er, the ocean. Floundering in the deep blue sea, little Jonah instructed me: "Now you be the whale, Daddy."

I slithered from the couch and fashioned a giant whale's mouth with my arms. As I clapped my arms together like the jaws of a great white shark, I hunted my little prey and chanted, "Here comes the big whale to eat up Jonah!"

Suddenly the game stopped. Bennett gave me one of those what-are-you-talking-about, how-dumb-can-you-get looks and informed me, "No, Daddy! The whale doesn't eat Jonah. He saves him."

At first I thought his comment was a two-year-old's trick to keep the mighty, tickling, whale arms from getting him. But with a moment's reflection, I saw the truth of his words.

I'd been to seminary. I had taken a course on the minor prophets. I even knew some Hebrew. I could explain to you the varied history of scholarly interpretation of the Book of Jonah. I thought I knew this prophet's story pretty well. But it took a toddler to show me how I'd always misread the meaning of the whale.

The way I'd always read this story, Jonah was rebellious and God was angry. The Lord, in His righteousness, sent a big fish to swallow him until he repented. I'd always thought of the whale as part of the punishment. I figured the whale was kind of a giant time-out for the strong-willed prophet: "Here, Jonah, sit in the middle of these whale guts by yourself for a few days. Maybe you'll come to your senses."

But that's not the way the story reads at all. Little Bennett was right. The whale's role was simple: Keep the poor prophet from drowning. When Jonah was inside the big fish, he didn't pray, "Oh God, I'm being eaten by this killer fish. Help me, Lord, before I become whale cud." Instead, the prophet's prayer was an expression of gratitude: "The engulfing waters threatened me, the deep surrounded me.... I sank down.... But you brought my life up from the pit" (Jonah 2:5–6).

God liked Jonah's prayer of thanksgiving and ordered the fish to spit Jonah onto the beach. My boy was right. The big fish didn't eat Jonah; it saved him.

There's a whale of a difference between being eaten and being saved, isn't there?

Look back over your life. Have you ever mistaken a saving whale for a man-eating shark? Have you ever faced a circumstance that, at the time, seemed like it was going to consume you—only to realize later that it helped deliver you? Maybe your heart was broken by an old boyfriend. At the time you thought God must hate you. But, now, married to the man of your dreams, you thank God daily for ending that old, going-nowhere romance. Maybe your whale was a company's downsizing that threatened personal ruin but instead resulted in your finding a much better job.

*O*f course, God is not mocked. He still grants us free will. Yes, He will eventually allow those who reject Him to drown in sin. The Bible is clear: Many will ultimately be separated from God for eternity (Romans 6:23). Tragically, a lot of people will miss the great wedding party because of their stubbornness (Matthew 22:4–5).

But I still can't believe how patient God is toward His rebellious beloved. Imagine Jesus standing at the door of your heart and knocking. How do you picture the scene? I'd always imagined a meek Jesus tapping gently with one knuckle. But the more I consider His passionate pursuit of me, I see a different mental picture. This diligent Suitor is not the kind who leaves the front porch after one polite knock. It's not *tap, tap, tap.* "Okay, I'll be on my way."

No, Jesus knocks with both fists, for He is a Suitor in love.

He'll do what it takes. He'll send you a dozen roses every day until you finally enjoy the aroma of holiness. He'll send you love letters every week until you acknowledge the authority of His Word. He'll stand beneath your bedroom window and sing ballads with angels until you notice there's a heavenly choir in your life. He'll cry out at midnight, wake up the neighbors, and rouse you from your slumber until you finally poke your head out the window of your soul to hear His voice.

Does such a picture of Jesus disturb you? It's humbling for a suitor to keep seeking his beloved despite her rejections. It's belittling when your date hides in the bathroom just to avoid dancing with you. Does it bother you to consider the sovereign God of the universe banging so hungrily at the door of His

LOVER OF MY SOUL

beloved? Is it unsettling to watch the King of Kings keep calling despite His beloved's repeated cold shoulder, rejection, and scorn?

The picture should disturb you and astound you. To feel the fullness of His affection, you must ponder the humility of this Messiah, "Who, being in very nature God, did not consider equality with God something to be grasped, but made himself nothing" (Philippians 2:6–7). Do you see it?

No one has ever wanted you as much as this heavenly Husband.

Watch. He's sending you whale-sized lifeboats every day— you might as well climb aboard. Listen. He's singing beneath your window—you might as well come out and drink in the music. Look. He's extending His hand again—you might as well join Him on the dance floor. This Suitor's not going to give up on you. He'll turn a deaf ear to all your rejections until you say yes. I'm not sure He can even hear you when you say no.

CHAPTER THREE

A MARRIAGE MADE IN HEAVEN

"Father, I want those you have given me...."
John 17:24

ete's the kind of unpretentious, delightful Christian who figures that if God spoke to Abraham and Moses and Paul, then God can certainly speak to him.

Pete said God told him to go on a fast. So he did. After he began, Pete figured that there must be a reason for the fast— some issue to resolve or some decision to make. But what? Oh yeah, Pete remembered that he wasn't married, and he wasn't getting any younger. He decided to ask God for a mate.

He had met some young ladies through the singles group at his church. So after fasting several days, Pete started listing potential wives before the Lord.

"Is it Suzy, Lord?" Nothing in his heart stirred, so he figured it wasn't Suzy. "Is it Caroline, Lord?" Nothing. "Tamara? No? Whew, I'm glad it's not Tamara." As you can imagine, the list started shrinking. At this pace Pete would soon run out of names. So he started mentioning mere acquaintances.

"Is it Jean?" Pete had briefly met Jean weeks before. Their meetings since then had totaled about fifteen minutes. Pete wasn't sure if Jean would even remember him. But when he mentioned her name to the Lord, his heart thumped. So he asked again, "God, is it Jean?" His heart raced. His blood pumped as if someone had flipped an electrical switch in his soul. "It's Jean, isn't it, Lord? It's Jean! I'm supposed to marry Jean Llorens."

Pete was so positive about the answer to his prayers that he called two friends that day and told them: "I'm going to marry Jean Llorens. I just wanted you to be a witness to it."

A few days later Pete showed up at the church office where Jean worked, gave her a dozen roses, and asked her out. On their third date, he announced as calmly and plainly as unpretentious Pete knew how that the Lord had told him they were supposed to get married.

I'd like to have seen her face. You can imagine the tone of her response: "When the Lord tells me the same thing, we'll talk about it."

In time God did.

As Pete finished telling me the story, Joy and Renee, their infant twins, were waking up. Their one-year-old, Marie, was helping hug the babies. Dinner was ready. I smiled and shook my head in disbelief at Jean, who enjoyed hearing the story again because she knew it was all true. Who says one-liners and nervous phone calls are the only way to find a mate? Who says "playing the field" is the only way to play the game?

Actually the whole dating game as we know it was virtually unheard of until the twelfth or thirteenth century, when romantic courtship became popular. Before then almost all marriages were prearranged.

If you had been a young Hebrew man or woman in Jesus'

time, your dad probably would have selected your mate for you. Sometimes the father would use a third party called a *shadkan*— a matchmaker—to arrange the marriage. Unfortunately, over time the professional matchmaker developed a scandalous reputation as a charlatan flesh trader.

But the roots of the Hebrew matchmaker are beautiful and noble. You'll find the shadkan's origin in Genesis 24.

> *[Abraham] said to the chief servant in his household..., "...I want you to swear...that you will not get a wife for my son from the daughters of the Canaanites...but will go to my country and my own relatives and get a wife for my son Isaac."* (Genesis 24:2–4)

You can understand the mind of Abraham and the urgency in his voice. God had promised the patriarch a nation. All of Israel's future lay dormant in Abraham's boy. Isaac's marriage could not be built upon whimsy; the matchmaker's work was vital.

When the servant came to the town of Nahor, he stopped at the community well and prayed a prayer similar to Pete's:

> *"O LORD, God of my master Abraham, give me success today.... May it be that when I say to a girl, 'Please let down your jar that I may have a drink,' and she says, 'Drink, and I'll water your camels too'—let her be the one you have chosen for your servant Isaac."* (Genesis 24:12, 14)

Rebekah answered the matchmaker's request, "Drink, my lord" (Genesis 24:18) and then added, "I'll draw water for your camels too" (Genesis 24:19). What a way to find a wife!

But the shadkan's job wasn't over once the right match was made. In the first place, the woman and her family had to agree to the match. Abraham had told his servant at the outset, "If the woman is unwilling to come back with you, then you will be released from this oath of mine" (Genesis 24:8). Although the groom's father took initiative in finding a bride, the maiden was never coerced into the marriage.

The prearranged marriage sure didn't stifle romance for Rebekah and Isaac. Godly Hebrew couples enjoyed the beauty of infatuated, exhilarating passion. Read the Song of Songs. The Israelites knew about a love that "burns like blazing fire, like a mighty flame. Many waters cannot quench love; rivers cannot wash it away" (Song of Songs 8:6–7). Prearranged union didn't hinder real love for the people of God. In fact, it granted opportunity for the truest love of all. It was a love seated in choice, rooted in commitment. It was unconditional love boiled down to its essence. It was loving someone just because he or she was yours.

Isn't that what we crave? Don't you long for someone to love you not because of the size of your bank account or the size of your waist? Oh, for the love that is built upon this simple assurance: "My lover is mine and I am his" (Song of Songs 2:16).

Will teenagers quit dating? Probably not. Dating's fun. Should we employ matchmakers? I doubt my boy would ever agree to it. So what's my point? When the Scripture writers were inspired to call you the bride of Christ, they weren't thinking of the American way of marriage. They were thinking of the old, Jewish way. Prearranged marriage. Get the picture yet? Let me paint it plainly.

A Father named Jehovah had an unmarried Son. When the time was right, the Father didn't shirk His responsibility to find His Son a bride. He sent His Spirit into the world to woo, pursue, and win a bride for the Prince of Peace. The Matchmaker found you. The price for your hand was set. The arrangements were etched into a covenant of grace. The bride price was paid at Calvary.

Now, gentleman-like, the Father awaits your consent. With just the nod of your head and a sip from His cup, the Father will smile and present you to the Groom.

*P*lease grab hold of this life-changing truth and never let go. It explains why Jesus wants you. It explains why He has pursued you so persistently. It is your ticket to freedom from the tyranny of performance.

Jesus wants you not because of the way you wear your hair or the cute little way you walk. He wants you not because you have a great sense of humor or because you're so successful. He wants you not because you clean house so well or because you run the corporation so efficiently. He wants you not because you attend church so faithfully or because you teach Sunday school so energetically.

The Son wants you for one reason: The Father gave you to Him. "Father, I want those you have given me to be with me where I am" (John 17:24). No one comes to Jesus except the Father draws him (John 6:44). From eternity the Father pointed past a million galaxies to you on planet Earth and declared, "There she is, Son. Your Bride. Go love her."

So Christ did.

Don't miss the importance of the Father's big setup. Jesus' affection for you is not flippant. His love for you will never wither. He loves you more deeply, more enduringly than the human mind can comprehend.

After all, it's a marriage made in heaven.

CHAPTER FOUR

THE BRIDE FROM THE BROTHEL

"Go, take to yourself an adulterous wife."
Hosea 1:2

The young evangelist, a highly eligible bachelor and powerful preacher, attracted the attention of the church ladies. Many women may have hoped for a date with the nationally known communicator, but everyone knew he wouldn't marry until God told him when—and who.

I imagine he, like all men, thought about getting married. I'm sure he wanted to feel a woman's affection, longed for a partner who would share his life and his vision, wanted a helpmate to walk through the valleys with him and to smile as together they navigated the precipices. I'm sure he prayed that God would give him a wonderful wife.

Then one day out of the blue, God spoke to the preacher. *It's time for you to get married. I have selected you a wife.*

Like an exuberant child, the man of God thrust his fist in the air, did a little victory dance, and shouted, "YES!"

"Who is it, Lord?" the preacher began to ponder. "Is it Samantha in the choir? The one with that beautiful voice—ahh, what a sweet melody comes from her mouth. Is she the one, Lord? I could make beautiful harmony with her."

No. She is not in the choir.

"Oh, well," the minister conceded. "Is it Mary Jo, the new secretary? I don't know her very well yet, but she's beautiful, and I know she's a good administrator. I could use a wife with a good sense of details. Is it she?"

No. She is not in the church at all.

"Not in the church? Oh, she's in another church. Okay, I can handle that. What denomination is she? Is it that woman with the red hair I met at the Christian bookstore the other day?"

No. She's not in any church.

"What do you mean, Lord, 'not in any church'? Where would she be? Where might I find her then?"

Go downtown, past the old depot, next to the abandoned warehouse. You'll see an old store with a red light that says "All Girl Staff." She's in there.

The preacher grew silent. Surely he hadn't heard God correctly. "Lord, my future wife couldn't be there. That's the worst part of town!"

She's there.

"But Lord, I can't even be seen in a place like that! It's a house of ill repute. It's a brothel! What would the parishioners say if they found out I'd gone there? What would my future wife be doing in a brothel? Is she a missionary? A social worker? What is she?"

She's a harlot. Now, "Go, take to yourself an adulterous wife."

True story! Those were God's actual words, recorded in Hosea 1:2. "Go, take to yourself an adulterous wife." You can imagine what the young preacher felt. Hosea's whole prophetic career was on the line. His credibility was at stake. His burgeoning ministry could fall to scandal.

What happened next is only half of a verse in the Bible but is more than half the secret of the Christian life: simple obedience. The scripture simply reports: "So [Hosea] married Gomer" (Hosea 1:3).[1]

*H*osea had to marry Gomer in order to understand what it was like for God to seek out and wed Himself to the people of Israel. I suppose I'd have to marry a harlot in order to comprehend what it was like for Jesus to invite me to the altar. From eternity the Son awaited His Father's order. When time was full, the heavenly Father declared, *I have a bride for You.*

"Where is she, Father? What pure companion awaits? Have You created another Adam and Eve, another Garden of Eden? Where is this pure, undefiled fellowship You have chosen for the Son of God?"

There. God pointed toward the rebellious planet. He pointed at the people who had eaten forbidden fruit. He pointed at the people who had danced around golden calves. He pointed at those who had made pleasure their greatest passion. He pointed at all the people who had sold themselves cheaply and thoughtlessly for a quick dime or a quick thrill. He pointed at pornographers, drug pushers, pimps, and felonious prisoners. He pointed at the self-righteous, the self-absorbed, the lukewarm. He pointed at corrupt government leaders. He pointed at people who harbored private sins. He pointed at you and me.

There is your bride, Son. Go, take to yourself an adulterous wife.

So the Word became flesh, and He betrothed Himself to you and to me.

The real miracle was not that Hosea married Gomer. That was simple obedience. The real miracle was that, somehow, the prophet loved the harlot. He looked at her hardened face, her overdone makeup and gaudy clothes and somehow saw beyond her vile exterior. He knew her repeated promiscuity had left her with venereal diseases. But somehow he still took her home to his own bed.

The real marvel is not that Jesus came to save the lost. That also was simple obedience. The marvel is that He loved those He came to save. The miracle is not that He came to a spiritually adulterous generation. The miracle is that He actually adored His bride whom He took from the brothel.

osea took Gomer by the hand and led her out the grimy front door as the red light flashed above their heads. He escorted her to the car and opened the door for her. No man had ever opened a door for the prostitute before. He took her to the finest restaurant in town. He put a solitaire on her finger. She kept examining it closely, unable to believe it was a real diamond. Hosea had to show her the receipt just to prove that it came from the jewelry store, not the bubble gum machine. She hardly spoke at dinner, for no man had ever loved her before. No man had ever treated her this way.

Because Gomer had never been treated so well, she figured it was too good to be true. Her husband promised to provide for her and protect her, but she couldn't believe it. "Why do you love me?" Gomer asked over and over. "Why would a holy prophet like you love a filthy outcast like me?"

"I love you because I love you," Hosea would say. "You are my wife. I love you just because you are mine."

She couldn't understand it. Hosea didn't pay her for her services like the men back at the brothel did. All she had ever known was prostitution. Give a man what he wants, and he gives you what you want. Gomer couldn't believe Hosea's love would last. She couldn't trust that he would always be there for her.

One day Hosea had gone to the temple to prophesy. It was close to dinnertime, and Gomer was hungry. She went to the marketplace to buy some bread. While she browsed nervously among the bakery stands, one of her former "customers" spotted her. "Why, Gomer," he said, "what are you doing shopping for your food? You look hungry. How about letting me buy your dinner?"

Gomer trembled. She thought of Hosea. No telling when he would come home. He might never come back for her, and she was hungry. So she nodded her head yes, knowing what it meant. The customer smiled that perverse, knowing grin she had seen on hundreds of men's faces for more than a decade. He led her to a nearby alley. It was dark and smelled of rotting produce and urine. The dirty man was rough with her. But she had learned over the years not to think or resist. She had conditioned herself to feel nothing. Her emotions were numb, her heart callous.

Afterward the customer gave her enough money to buy a small loaf of bread. As he walked away, he chuckled, "Let me know if you ever get hungry again."

*W*hen Hosea returned home after a full day of preaching, his bride was gone. Listen to Hosea crying out: "Gomer!" *Where is she?* "Gomer, my beloved, where are you?" Hosea kept posing the question to the night air. "Where are you, beloved? Where are you?" He asked because he loved her. He asked because he wanted her back. He asked because his heart ached with the pain of her absence. But in his heart the prophet knew his wife had returned to the brothel.

Where are you? It's the first question God ever asked His beloved (Genesis 3:9). He asked because He loved Adam. He asked because His own heart hurt to see His beloved hiding in shame. He asked because He wanted Adam and Eve restored.

Where are you? God's not asking because He's wondering. He's asking because He wants you in His loving arms. He asks because He misses you. He asks because He knows and desires what's best for you. Where is your heart? Where are you looking for bread?

Yet, it was easier for Gomer to make a quick dime as an adulteress than to trust the promised provisions of her husband. She said, 'I will go after my lovers, who give me my food and my water, my wool and my linen, my oil and my drink'" (Hosea 2:5).

Why is it so hard for us to accept God's love? Why is grace so hard to receive?

Gomer retreated to adultery because she thought it would provide for her immediate need. It was all she knew. She couldn't believe life could be different. She couldn't comprehend how a man could love—really love—as Hosea said he loved her. Her husband had given her new clothes, a new name, a new home,

THE BRIDE FROM THE BROTHEL
THE BRIDE FROM THE BROTHEL

and a new future. But when her husband was gone for a few hours, she still went back to the brothel.

If God seems momentarily absent, remember: He is not. His promise is sound, His provision sure. If His love seems too good to be true, remember: It's real. It's complete. When life is momentarily difficult, you might be tempted to retreat to your spiritual brothel. It might be a besetting sin or an old lust or just plain apathy. But before you take the first step toward your old red-light district, ask yourself: *Has spiritual compromise ever made me feel more alive?*

*I*t's incomprehensible that God didn't give up on Israel, and me, and you. Despite Israel's spiritual infidelity, the Lord decided to woo her back. "Therefore I am now going to allure her; I will lead her into the desert and speak tenderly to her" (Hosea 2:14).

Imagine it. The humiliated husband plans to court his unfaithful wife. God wanted Hosea to understand this unbelievable divine love. So the Lord instructed the prophet: "Go, show your love to your wife again, though she is loved by another and is an adulteress. Love her as the LORD loves the Israelites, though they turn to other gods" (Hosea 3:1).

*W*hen Hosea went to the brothel to rescue his wife, the madam in charge put a bodyguard in front of Gomer and declared that the woman would not be released unless Hosea bought her.

"Buy her?" Hosea stuttered. "But she's already my wife!" He

thought about flinging himself against the bodyguard and taking Gomer by force. The prophet was a strong man. He probably could have handled the brute. Instead, he reached into his pouch and pulled out the money. "So I bought her for fifteen shekels of silver and about a homer and a lethek of barley" (Hosea 3:2).

Buying back. That's what *redeem* means. Of course it's humbling to buy back what is already yours. But crosses are meant to be humbling. So Hosea stepped into the brothel, reached into his pocketbook, and paid for the wife he'd already wed.

If you are a Christian, you are twice God's. You're His because He married you, and you're His because He paid a price for you. God is a Husband who "forgives all your sins" but also "redeems your life from the pit" (Psalm 103:3–4).

If Hosea could redeem his bride from the brothel, what pit is so deep that God cannot redeem you? If Hosea could love a prostitute wife who returned to her harlotry, what mistake of yours could keep you from God's love?

Gomer put her hand in Hosea's, hung her head, and followed him back out that same grimy door under that same red, flashing light. As before, Hosea opened the car door for her. Once inside the car, the unfaithful wife spoke without lifting her head. "Okay, Hosea, you've bought me. I'm yours. I'm your servant. What do you want me to do for you?"

Hosea spoke tenderly. "You don't understand, beloved. I didn't buy you because I needed you to serve me. I bought you because I love you. I wanted you, and it was the only way to get you back." Perhaps then the prophet echoed the Word of the Lord: "you will call me 'my husband'; you will no longer call me 'my master'" (Hosea 2:16).

"What, then, do you want from me?" Gomer asked.

"Your love," Hosea said. "I want you to treat me as your husband instead of as a customer. I know how you sought to please them just so they would pay you. I want your heart to beat with passion toward me. I want your soul to stir and your whole body to tingle at my touch. I want your passion and your affection and your whole attention. Love is all I want, my beloved. Love."

The longer I'm with God, the more amazed I am that He wanted me. I'm not sure which is more astounding, that He saved me or that He keeps forgiving me. I'm the bride God plucked from the brothel. No matter how shallow or deep your sin, you're from the brothel too. That's why we must ask: "You bought me, God. You own me fair and square. What then do you want from me, Lord?"

Listen closely. His answer is clear: *Love the Lord your God with all your heart, with all your soul, and with all your strength.*

CHAPTER FIVE

THE COST OF A DIAMOND

You were bought at a price.
1 Corinthians 7:23

e hadn't been engaged long. Anne didn't know I was watching while she stared at her new ring. She rotated her hand under the lamplight, observing the diamond from different angles. At first I wondered if she was checking for imperfections or bubble gum residue. But then I saw her smile. She was looking at her diamond because it made *her* feel like a diamond. The more it sparkled, the more her own face glowed.

"Whatcha doing?" I surprised her.

She blushed. "Just looking."

I didn't poke any further, though it might have been fun. It was a precious sight, a bride looking at the symbol of her groom's affection. "Just looking" at what he had spent for the privilege of asking her to marry him.

You ought to take a good long look at what Christ gave to get you.

We give rings. In biblical times a groom might have given a lot more. Abraham's servant gave Rebekah "gold and silver jewelry and articles of clothing…; he also gave costly gifts to her brother and to her mother" (Genesis 24:53). I wonder if Rebekah ever held her wrists under the lantern just to watch the bracelets shine. Jacob worked seven years on his father-in-law's farm for the right to marry Rachel. I wonder if Rachel ever stared at Jacob in the field and thought about the years he labored to wed her.

The Hebrew people regarded the bride price as a vital part of the marriage arrangement. It wasn't, by any means, a man buying a woman. But the betrothal agreement always included a gift from the groom's family to the bride's. It let the bride know her groom was committed. More importantly, it let her know she was worth it.

*T*he words are well-worn but seem no worse for the wear. They became the lyrics to a song, and they still paint a picture so poignant that a preacher can't resist repeating Myra Brooks Welch's "The Touch of the Master's Hand." I invite you, right now, to sit back, shoo away any distractions, and read this wonderful poem aloud. Enjoy its meter and metaphor. But listen carefully. There's something amiss in these touching verses:

> *'Twas battered and scarred, and the auctioneer*
> *Thought it scarcely worth his while*
> *To waste much time on the old violin,*
> *But he held it up with a smile.*
> *"What am I bidden, good folks?" he cried.*
> *"Who'll start the bidding for me?*
> *A dollar, a dollar"—then, "Two! Only two?*
> *Two dollars, and who'll make it three?*
> *Three dollars, once; three dollars, twice;*

going for three—" But no,
From the room, far back, a gray-haired man
Came forward and picked up the bow;
Then, wiping the dust from the old violin,
And tightening the loose strings,
He played a melody pure and sweet
As a caroling angel sings.

The music ceased, and the auctioneer,
With a voice that was quiet and low,
Said, "What am I bidden for the old violin?"
And he held it up with the bow.
"A thousand dollars, and who'll make it two?
Two thousand! And who'll make it three?
Three thousand, once; three thousand, twice;
And going, and gone!" said he.
The people cheered, but some of them cried,
"We do not quite understand.
What changed its worth?" Swift came the reply:
"The touch of the master's hand."

And many a man with life out of tune,
And battered and scarred with sin,
Is auctioned cheap to the thoughtless crowd,
Much like the old violin.
A mess of pottage, a glass of wine;
A game—and he travels on.
He's "going" once, and "going" twice,
He's "going" and "almost gone."

But the Master comes, and the foolish crowd
Never can quite understand
The worth of a soul, and the change that's wrought
By the touch of the Master's hand.

Myra Welch's poem has all the ingredients to qualify as a preacher's delight. Its meter is simple, its rhyme readable. It rivets the listener by painting a vivid word picture. The element of surprise stirs the imagination. The simplicity of the parallel makes the image linger.

So what's wrong?

It's so subtle you may have never noticed it. I quoted the poem many times before I spotted it. I've been too taken by the great truths in the verses to notice their one mistake.

After all, who hasn't felt like a worn-out, warped instrument whose music was lost along the way? Who hasn't wondered if his worth has withered with time? Who hasn't wondered if her value has decreased as her age has increased? The stirring poem has the hope of conversion. Like a tear-filled testimony, the rhyme teaches that hope has its reasons and real change is possible. We are not doomed to stay as we are. The Master Musician who made us knows how to play us. And life's melody does become oh so sweet when we are touched by the Master's hand.

What possibly could be wrong with the metaphor painted in the famous lyrics?

It's the sequence that's wrong. It's backward.

The master played the instrument, and then the high price was paid. The violin was tuned and *then* called a treasure. The violin showed its worth and *then* was deemed a collector's item.

But that's not the way a groom takes a bride. The bride price is paid long before the wife proves her value. The expensive ring is purchased first. Then the wedding is planned.

Consider how you became like a Stradivarius. You didn't get touched by God and *then* become a treasure. You didn't become valuable *after* God began producing fruit in you. Christ bought you before you'd proven your worth. You weren't used by God and *then* blessed greatly. You were blessed greatly and *then* used by God.

God labels His children heroes before they ever act nobly. He calls us saints before we ever act holy. He calls us champions before we ever win the race.

Hard to believe? Consider one Bible hero.

For seven years the Midianites had been terrorizing the Israelites. There wasn't anything especially powerful about the pagan army. But the Hebrew people were cowering in clefts and caves. They were crouching in every crook and cranny they could find. And while the Israelites hid, the Midianites helped themselves to all the Hebrew sheep, cattle, and crops.

God wasn't pleased with His sniveling soldiers. But He decided to do something about the Midianites anyway.

An angel visited a man named Gideon, who was threshing wheat.

I can't explain the finer details of the art of wheat threshing (and I'm sure you're glad I can't). Here's what's important: Threshing was an outdoor chore. An outdoor ox pulled an outdoor sledge. The outdoor wind blew away the chaff. But

Gideon wasn't outdoors on the threshing floor. He was closed up in a winepress. It was probably a hollow carved in rock. A winepress was a good place for squashing grapes and a good place for hiding. But it was no place to beat out wheat.

Why was Gideon in the winepress with his wheat? The Bible says "to keep it from the Midianites" (Judges 6:11). But wheat wasn't the only thing Gideon wanted to keep from the Midianites. He wanted to keep himself from them.

While he was hiding with his wheat, "the angel of the LORD appeared to Gideon [and] said, 'The LORD is with you, mighty warrior'" (Judges 6:12).

"Mighty warrior"?

Wait a minute. Review the scene. The man is hiding in a hole in the rock. Cowering in a cave, wheezing over wheat chaff, trembling in his sandals, looking over his shoulder, groveling for bread—this man is a "mighty warrior"? Marines on Iwo Jima, Schwarzkopf in the Gulf War—those are mighty warriors. But Gideon was a sniveling, play-it-safe, you're-not-going-to-get-my-wheat-or-me kind of guy.

It just proves that God doesn't wait for His bride to glow before He gives her a sparkling diamond.

He didn't wait for Adam and Eve to become productive before He affirmed them. He blessed Adam and Eve and then said, "Be fruitful and multiply." God didn't wait for Abraham to start multiplying before commissioning him. The Lord blessed Abraham, saying, "Your seed will be as the stars in the sky." *Then* He sent the patriarch onward. Jehovah blessed Moses from the bush *then* sent him to Pharaoh. He blessed Jeremiah in his mother's womb and *then* appointed him a prophet unto the nations. He called Simon "the Rock" *before* Peter ever preached a real sermon.

Ponder it. You may not have licked even the smallest of your bad habits yet, but the Lord has called you more than a conqueror (Romans 8:37). You may have a bouncing bank account, but God has called you spiritually rich (Ephesians 1:7–8). You may not even wear a bathrobe gracefully, but the King of Kings has adorned you with a royal mantle (1 Peter 2:9).

Do you see what's amiss in the poem now? With God, the buying precedes the using. The purchasing precedes the playing. The high price comes first. Then comes the beautiful music.

The familiar poem should read differently to tell the tale rightly. Instead of first rising to play the old instrument, the master would have raised his hand in the auction. "Three thousand!" he would have shouted. No, "Three million!" Whatever the figure, it would have been all he had. And then, having declared the violin worth everything, he would have taken it in his hands—and proven it worth every dime he'd paid for it.

It's the difference between the ways of the world and the way of God. The world waits to see you prove your worth, then calls you wonderful. God blesses you and then watches your life become beautiful to fulfill the promise of His words. God buys you with His blood, then lets the world see how brightly you can shine.

The proof of the Groom's love is as close as a rotating hand under the lamplight. It's not your hand though. It's the Messiah's.

Watch it turn. There! See the nail holes? Don't be in a hurry. The price He paid proves your worth. Take time to consider it all again. If anyone catches you pondering Calvary, tell them you're "just looking" at your diamond.

CHAPTER SIX

GOD'S BEAUTY TREATMENTS

...six months with oil of myrrh and six
with perfumes and cosmetics.
Esther 2:12

nne and I once vacationed with my brother and his wife at a posh ski resort. There was plenty to do—skiing, indoor swimming, and bowling. Our wives tolerated our athletic activities, but they didn't come home talking about the lifts, the laps, or the lanes. Their real fun was the beauty spa.

It's hard for me to imagine someone voluntarily signing up for the beauty spa, much less paying large sums of money for the experience. What could be fun about having a stranger scrape, file, and polish your toenails for an hour? I don't like to clip my own toenails; I sure don't want to sit in a chair and watch Oprah while someone else tinkers with my tootsies. Besides, the indelible polish has a pungent odor strong enough to singe a husband's nostril hairs. The odor lasts just about the length of time that a woman wears the polish before deciding to change colors. It then requires battery acid to remove the old polish.

And my wife and sister-in-law had more in mind than pedicures during their day at the spa. Their beautification treatments began with a massage. A massage sounds pretty good, but you've got to be suspicious of any therapist who begins by saying, "Now this won't hurt a bit…" I have visions of a black-belt martial artist chopping on my vertebrae. Of course, I've never had a professional massage, so I wouldn't know. Even at a high-class health facility, I can't get past the fear of news reaching my hometown paper: *Presbyterian Pastor Frequents Massage Parlor.* From her description of her masseuse, I imagined Anne's rubdown was administered by an aging World War II torture specialist named Ulga.

The women's next "treatment" was a mineral bath. The mountainous resort became famous for its mineral springs years ago when old, sick politicians visited to soak their sagging bodies in the allegedly healing pools. People have been visiting the waters ever since with hopes of being restored and revitalized. Now I'm no expert on communicable diseases, but it seems to me that if you want healing, you should avoid little pools of water that have had thousands of old, sick people sitting in them for fifty years. Nonetheless, the women enjoyed their soaking.

They called their next luxurious therapy a "salt glow," a dubious procedure in which salt is rubbed over the body. Reportedly, the salty scouring helps cleanse the skin of impurities and exfoliates old, dead epidermal cells. Wouldn't a Black & Decker sander on a low setting give the same results? Besides, isn't a salt rub what a taxidermist gives a freshly skinned animal hide?

Our wives' posh spa extravaganza concluded with the most puzzling therapy of all. I've forgotten the clinical name for the procedure; I just remember it as the "water pelting." For her spa finale, my wife was asked to strip and stand against the wall in a long, tiled room. While my naked wife stood at one end of the overgrown shower stall, Ulga stood at the other end with a fire hose. I'm not sure how long the pelting lasted. I suppose the therapist continued the water torture until Anne confessed several U.S. military secrets.

My brother and I were glad we had all gone to the slopes and ballroom before our wives' spa adventure. After their rubs, scrubs, soaks, and peltings, our better halves were far too tired to join the common folk for such things as skiing and dancing. After their trip to the spa, about all they could do was sit there and be beautiful.

Though I make light of the ladies' search for beauty, I must admit there is someone else who also cares about a woman's beauty—her husband. This appreciation of female beauty is nothing new among men. It dates back to the Garden of Eden when God saw that Adam had no suitable partner and decided to take part of the man's strong side and make it into something lovely. When Adam saw the incredible creature, he said, "Wow!" (my translation). A husband's desire for his wife to be beautiful is not bad in and of itself, I suppose. Abraham, Isaac, and Jacob all regarded their wives as beautiful (see Genesis 12:11; 26:7; 29:17). But some husbands carry the simple desire to disgusting extremes.

King Xerxes gave all beauty-loving husbands a bad name. The Persian king, who reigned five centuries before Christ was born, threw a big bash to impress his friends. He showed off all his wealth and accomplishments, and then to top it off, he summoned his wife to display her beauty. But Queen Vashti refused to strut her stuff in front of the nobles. Hooray for her!

I'm glad she felt like being her husband's wife rather than his trophy. However, such womanly defiance was not welcome in those days. Vashti could have lost her head. She did lose her throne.

So Xerxes, intent on finding another beauty to show off, dispatched commissioners to every province of the realm in search of the most beautiful woman in the world. Whoever was most beautiful in the king's eyes would be the next queen.

What ensued was King Xerxes' own personal Miss Persia contest in which he was the sole judge. Although the contestants had to be stunningly gorgeous before they were privileged to make so much as an appearance before the king, Xerxes wanted to take no chances. Can you believe this requirement? "Before a girl's turn came to go in to King Xerxes, she had to complete twelve months of beauty treatments prescribed for the women, six months with oil of myrrh and six with perfumes and cosmetics" (Esther 2:12).

Imagine! Twelve months of Ulga's scrubbings, soakings, and peltings.

It's one thing for a woman to seek beauty treatments for herself. It's quite another for a husband to insist she have them. A smart, loving husband doesn't meddle or try to spur his wife's pursuit of beauty.

*E*ven my most discreet attempts to enhance my wife's natural beauty tend to backfire. One time I ordered her some nightwear from the Victoria's Secret catalog. It *had* to come from a catalog. Somehow the thought of milling through silk teddies in a store, in the middle of the mall where all my parishioners shop, is unsettling to me. I don't want to chitchat with the moderator of the women's council in the lingerie checkout line.

So I ordered Anne's present from the catalog. And because it was a catalog purchase no one would ever see, I went all out. The black negligee was—how shall I say it?—skimpy. The purchase included black stockings. When Anne opened her gift, she gave me a mischievous glance and spoke quietly, "Honey, how nice." Then she glanced around the room as if a parishioner might be peeking in the window and tucked the garment back in its box.

Unfortunately when she later tried it on, Anne discovered I had ordered the wrong size. The next day we headed out to the post office to mail the items back. As I helped our one-year-old into the backseat of the station wagon, I set the gown and stockings on top of the car. I should have known better. A man should never assume that his memory can last more than forty-five seconds while getting a toddler into a car. More importantly, no man should ever put his wife's lingerie on top of the car when its packaging clearly states her name and address.

Needless to say, when we arrived at the post office, the apparel hadn't. I was concerned about losing the money I'd invested in the apparel. My wife was concerned about losing her reputation. Anne spoke quietly but firmly when she realized what had happened: "Alan, dear, do you realize that somewhere in the city of Durham, a provocative, black, lace-trimmed negligee is lying by the side of the road with my name and address on it?"

We retraced our tire tracks, scouring the roads in search of the package. Finally we found the separately packaged black stockings on a curbside in our neighborhood. The fact that it was in our neighborhood should have been good news because it probably meant that the slinky nightgown was also in our neighborhood. But it was not good news. The neighborhood we lived in at the time was just a little over a mile from the church I was then pastoring. Most of my neighbors were also parishioners. We never found the black negligee. I have a discomforting feeling that one of my former deacons had a good laugh and is keeping it as blackmail material. The whole event served to remind me: (1) how incompetent I can be at ordering catalog items; (2) how forgetful I can be, especially if the result is destined to be embarrassing; and (3) how even my most noble attempts to adorn my wife can be disastrous.

Husbands can buy their wives clothes and jewelry and spa visits, but no man can actually make his wife be more beautiful. The chin and cheekbones she brings into the marriage are the only ones she'll ever have. If her eyes are brown, they'll always be brown. It's quite disconcerting to see a man marry a woman whom he wants to change. A woman wants a husband who loves her just as she is; after all, that's what genuine love is all about.

A man should never try to remake his wife. That's what was so silly about Xerxes' twelve-month beauty treatment prescription. All the oils and gold in Persia couldn't actually change a woman's beauty. If a husband wants to make his wife more beautiful, he needs to be more than a wealthy ruler—he must be a Creator.

God is determined to have a lovely bride. Ezekiel's prophetic recounting of God's marriage to Israel explained it: "I dressed you in fine linen and covered you with costly garments. I adorned you with jewelry.... You became very beautiful and rose to be a queen" (Ezekiel 16:10–11, 13). John's revelation confirmed it: "I saw the Holy City, the new Jerusalem, coming down out of heaven from God, prepared as a bride beautifully dressed for her husband" (Revelation 21:2).

Of course it's not physical beauty God is after. It's inner splendor. Here is the one instance in which it is good that a husband wants to make his bride more splendid. It's good because Jesus Christ is the one Husband who can actually make His bride into whatever He wants her to be.

Consider Isaiah's words: "your Maker is your husband—the Lord Almighty is his name" (Isaiah 54:5). Think on it. While earthly husbands foolishly might try to make their wives more beautiful, the heavenly Husband can actually make His bride into something altogether more lovely. It's a staggering thought: The One who chose you as His bride is the One who made you.

It's great news. If your Maker is your Husband, it means you don't have to be beautiful before He'll marry you. You're clay in His hands—He can make you into something more glorious than you ever imagined. The Lord, unlike Xerxes, has no need to search out every province in hopes of finding a bride beautiful enough for the King of kings. Such a search would be futile, of course. None of us has enough personal beauty to please God. In fact, in and of ourselves, we're downright ugly compared to His splendor.

Aren't you glad that God isn't holding a cosmic beauty contest looking for the creature with the loveliest soul? Instead of looking for contestants to demonstrate their spiritual beauty, the heavenly

Bridegroom searches the earth for men and women who will simply say yes to His marriage proposal—and who will yield to His beauty treatments. God doesn't require that you be beautiful before you marry Him. But once you're His, He insists you become more holy every day. When He begins a good work in His bride, He plans to bring it to completion (Philippians 1:6).

Therefore, God's spiritual beauty spa isn't optional. Most of us need a good spiritual massage because we tend to get stiff-necked. Most of us need an exfoliating salt scrub because we tend to be callous toward His grace. Most of us need a good soaking bath in His Spirit because we tend to dry up inwardly. And, admit it: Who among us doesn't need a good, godly pelting from time to time to soften our stubborn hearts into holy submission?

I guess wives will always want to be beautiful, and foolishly, husbands will always try to help them be so. I can't tell you how much Xerxes spent on beauty treatments for his bride (I think my wife's one-day spa visit cost more than my first car). But it wasn't nearly what God spent to make His bride beautiful. Do you know the price God paid to make you lovely in His eyes? The cross. He was stripped bare so you would be adorned with righteousness. The scars that made Him ugly made you beautiful. The blood that stained Him made you spotless.

Quite an extravagant beauty treatment, isn't it? Twelve months with Ulga wouldn't even come close to doing that.

CHAPTER SEVEN

"GOD—PRETTY!"

Worship the LORD in the beauty of holiness!
Psalm 96:9, NKJV

*I*t was Thursday morning. Sunday was coming. I would be out of town Friday and Saturday. Somehow I had to cram in some solid biblical exegesis and crank out a meaningful message by Thursday afternoon. All I had penned was my title: "The Beauty of Holiness."

Doesn't really grab you, does it?

A seminary professor once chastised a student for turning in a sermon assignment with a boring title. "Sermon titles must be catchy and relevant," the teacher insisted. "Take this sermon home and bring it back with a new, grabbing title."

"How do I come up with a catchy title?" inquired the drab sermonizer.

"It's easy," the teacher responded. "Just imagine your sermon title is posted on a sign in front of your church. It's Sunday morning and a big bus full of people has stopped momentarily by your sign. You want a sermon title so catchy that all the people on the bus will want to jump off the Greyhound and run into your church. Think of it that way—I'm sure you'll create a good title."

The student left to ponder the matter. The next day he returned with his new title: "There's a Bomb on Your Bus!"

Sermon titles *should* be catchy, and more importantly, every sermon's content should be relevant. Everyone wants something to chew on—real life application. We're drawn toward book and sermon titles like "Ten Steps to..." or "Fifteen Keys of..." And guess what book category always sells big? Cookbooks—step-by-step recipes, telling you how to get something cooked up. That's what people want from their preacher too—the ingredients and instructions for a warm, delicious life.

I pondered these things in my heart as I contemplated my sermon text for the coming Sunday: "Worship the LORD in the beauty of holiness!" (Psalm 96:9, NKJV). I started by considering the word *beauty*. What's beautiful to me?

- the image of my bride as she stepped into the aisle on the first day of the best years of my life
- the eyes of a toddler wide with wonder
- Yellowstone canyon, with its ocher and deep auburn walls jutting downward to the generous riverbed welcoming the tumbling waterfall
- an eagle in flight against a cloudless sky
- a Jamaican reef with its underwater panorama of color, its schools of tropical fish dividing and yielding to my snorkeled face
- a full rainbow after a brief rain shower
- sunset as seen from a rickety deck rocker across dunes of swaying sea oats on Ocean Isle Beach
- a freshly mown fairway in the early morning (I had to say it.)
- the Blue Ridge Parkway in October, its autumn leaves at peak season painting the North Carolina mountains,

beheld from a picnic blanket in a field that's still green

- my baby boy, freshly bathed and diapered and fed, who has fallen asleep in his mother's arms, wearing a hint of a smile as if he dreams of playing with angels

I was ready to consider my subject again: "Worship the Lord in the beauty of holiness." Surely holiness is the most beautiful sight of all. I felt a sermon coming on. But wait, where were the practical, relevant points? What would be the meaty application of my message?

Surely I could find a catchy, relevant life application tucked inside the text. I read and reread the verse. I looked at the context and checked the Hebrew words. But as I strained for practical applications, I found no life recipe. I couldn't cook up anything. In fact, the harder I tried to be practical, the more frustrated I became. My sermon seemed stuck in the swamp of irrelevance.

Meanwhile, the stack of stuff-to-do on my desk screamed at me. The yellow sticky notes were hollering louder than my Bible. Refusing to surrender to the tyranny of the to-do list, I tossed in the towel, turned off the laptop, and announced to the staff: "I'm getting out of here! I'm going to the gardens."

The church I pastor is directly across the street from the most beautiful garden in our city. Years ago, the lovely, historic grounds were the site of a business tycoon's home. Now the old, stately mansion is a museum whose magnificent garden is open to the public free of charge.

I took only the essentials: Bible, pen, pad, and fresh-squeezed orangeade from the adjacent soda shop. I perched on a dew-wet bench overlooking the gardens. My spot afforded a panoramic view of the floral splendor. *How wonderful*, I thought. *And how foolish of me to have been so close and yet so far from this garden.* The summer was about over, and this was the first time I had stopped by to see its glory.

I had good intentions of digging up Bible verses, taking copious notes, and composing a sermon outline. But the orangeade started tasting especially delicious. And the garden started looking unusually beautiful. So I gave myself permission to do nothing more than sit and sip.

I sat. Unproductive. Unaware of my next appointment. Thoughtless about the crunch of time. Unconcerned about the blank pad on my lap.

And I sipped. Sometimes slurped. Not knowing I was drinking in a whole garden.

I observed the different flora. I watched some gardeners at work and considered how much time and care must be devoted to cultivate such beauty. But slowly, steadily, my observation grew into a gaze.

Do you know the difference between observation and a gaze? An observation is a fact-finding mission. "What is this plant?" "What kind of blossom is that?" "How is this garden watered?" Those are observation questions. A gaze is a deeper look—not for the purpose of discovering information but for the sake of enjoyment. A gaze is more like absorbing than observing. I gazed. And slowly, surely, I forgot about myself and my earthly demands and became lost in the garden.

That's when I began to hear from God.

Worship Me in the beauty of holiness. It is an invitation to more than an observation of the King's glorious throne. It is more than counting the number of jewels in His heavenly crown or measuring the dimensions of His temple. It is more than Hebrew exegesis or systematic theology. It is an invitation to gaze upon the Lord's loveliness, not for education, but for enjoyment.

I began to understand the psalmist's words. Worshiping the beauty of God's holiness is an opportunity to become lost in His splendor. It is not a life-application study designed to glean a three-step recipe for practical daily living. The gaze upon God is, dare I say it, an activity without practical purpose but of profound significance.

My impractical gaze upon the garden taught me something about worship. I didn't want anything from the garden. I asked no questions of its roses. I posed no theological dilemmas to its hibiscus. Nor did I ask any favors of the plants. I didn't look upon the greenery wondering if it was edible. I made no plans to clip roses and sell them at the mall.

No one can enjoy beauty and demand it be useful at the same time.

Isn't that the primary way we miss beauty? As soon as we place a selfish demand upon the beautiful sight, we lose sight of its glory. If a man could look upon a woman and admire her beauty without fantasizing about having her, there would be no lust. But when the beholding turns to using, it becomes sin.

It's fine to ask God for things. In fact, He has instructed us to do so. But too often we worshipers become like tourists at the Grand Canyon. With a 35 mm camera, a Polaroid, and a handycam, the tourist collects lots of slides, photos, and footage to show his friends back home. He sees the famous site through his viewfinders but misses the canyon's grandeur for lack of a long, slow, unhurried...gaze.

ow silly to miss the beauty for the sake of a souvenir to show off. No one looks at the orange hues of a dusk sky and says, "I've just got to get one of those for myself." No one looks at Niagara Falls and says, "I simply must have one like it in my backyard." Some things aren't meant to be captured or used. They are just for beholding.

Watch the way a new bride beholds her groom. When he comes into her presence, she stops what she's doing. She looks, she smiles...she gazes. She will, over the years, ask for a lot of help from her husband. She'll count on him to fix leaky faucets and fertilize the lawn. And she'll look to him for protection when there's a bump in the night. She will need him to help provide food for the table, and she'll sometimes need his shoulder as her crying pillow.

A good husband will gladly be all those things—an amateur plumber, a willing protector, a reliable provider, a welcoming pillow. But no husband enters a marriage with just his duties in mind. Though he may not mind his regularly assigned chores, a "honey-do" list is not what he wants most from his wife.

What does he want? Her gaze.

My greatest marital joy is my wife's finding joy in me. When she smiles softly at me across a candlelit table, or feels proud to be next to me in a crowd, or laughs at my jokes—when she really, truly enjoys me—I am most fulfilled.

God, the heavenly Bridegroom, delights in answering your

prayers, comforting your hurts, and protecting you from harm. But my garden visit reminded me, our Prince is not primarily useful—He is beautiful.

"What is the chief end of man?" asks Westminster Catechism's first question. The answer: "To glorify God and enjoy Him forever." Imagine that. God didn't create you primarily to learn something about Him or do something for Him. He made you to admire His splendor and enjoy His beauty.

*T*he morning sun moved higher in the sky. I recalled how, when our little Bennett was just learning to talk, my wife purchased a new outfit. It was a well-deserved, I'm-so-thankful-to-be-out-of-maternity-clothes shopping splurge. Bennett and I took her to pick up the purchased-and-altered garment at the store. While Anne went in the store, I waited in the car with Bennett.

"Mommy sure is pretty, isn't she?" I asked the boy in the backseat. He didn't reply.

However, when Anne returned with her purchase and we began driving away, little Bennett managed to put two words together. Unsolicited, the one-year-old spoke loudly enough for his mother to hear: "Mama—pretty!"

Anne spun her head around quickly and looked at the lad who had spun words of gold: "What did you say?"

Bennett repeated himself. "Mama—pretty!"

Her head then whirled toward me, a smile in her eyes. "Did you tell him to say that?"

I shook my head no.

Anne savored the moment.

Our next stop was the mall to run another errand. Once there, as we were strolling little Bennett, I decided to bring up the subject again. "Hey Bennett, Mommy sure is pretty, isn't she?"

Then more loudly and more emphatically than before, Bennett began proclaiming: "Mama—pretty! Mama—pretty!" As we strolled through the crowded mall, Bennett went before his mother announcing her splendor to anyone who had ears to hear: "Mama—pretty! Mama—pretty!" Meanwhile the pretty mama walked behind her boy, blushing but basking in the praise.

I left my garden bench and said good-bye to the roses and hibiscus. I had been there two hours. A little chuckle mixed with a sigh arose within as I said to myself, *This garden has been right across the street—ablaze with color all summer long—and I've missed it until now.* With resolve to come back soon and smell the roses again, I crossed the street to meet my next appointment.

Quietly, confidently, I realized I had my sermon. I had no catchy title and no practical life-application outline. But I had my sermon. I preached it Sunday. It went something like this: "God—pretty. God—pretty. God—pretty."

Did it ever occur to you that your heavenly Groom wooed you, courted you, and won you just so you could enjoy the beauty of His holiness? You don't need a flower garden across the street to see the beauty of the Rose of Sharon. Open the Word—you'll see the Splendor there. Open your heart—you can behold the Beauty. Open your mouth—you were created to proclaim it: "God—pretty. Holiness—beautiful."

WON

True Hero

Betrothed

Just Married

Taking His Name

Knowing Him

Sweet Somethings in Your Ear

CHAPTER EIGHT

TRUE HERO

Thanks be to God! He gives us the victory.
1 Corinthians 15:57

lizabeth took her seat on the F train, commuting to her Brooklyn home after another honest day's work. An attractive man across the car caught her eye. But her gaze was interrupted suddenly as a subway thief snatched the gold necklace off Elizabeth's neck.

I doubt she was shocked to get mugged on a New York subway. But she was bound to have been stunned by what she saw next. The attractive stranger she'd noticed leaped to his feet and dashed after the crook. Elizabeth watched her mugger and her hero disappear into the crowd, wondering if she'd ever see either again.

Elizabeth told everyone she knew the story, looking for clues to her hero's whereabouts. Her search lasted months. When she figured she'd never find her pendant or her prince, Elizabeth got another shock.

One night she was hanging out with friends at a local restaurant when the waiter brought her a glass of white wine and pointed at a man across the room. There—sparkling and dancing in the bottom of the wine glass—was her stolen necklace. And, there he was—standing and smiling in front of her—her hero.

"I grabbed it from the man who stole it," he said. "I've carried it with me everywhere hoping to meet you again."[1]

Everyone loves a hero.

The damsel in distress is doomed unless her knight in shining armor storms the evil king's castle. The city of Gotham is lost to Cat Woman's claws unless the Caped Crusader responds to Commissioner Gordon's bat signal in the midnight sky. The world will melt under nuclear holocaust unless 007 infiltrates the enemy's fortress and decodes the atomic detonator in time.

Maybe we crave comic book stories and James Bond movies because, deep down, we all need a hero. Though we feign self-sufficiency, we're thrilled to watch a real rescue. Though we pretend to be strong, we're dazzled by the sight of real power. Despite our brave facades, we're spellbound by real courage. Some might manage a calm exterior, but inwardly most of us are like damsels in distress. Something's been lost, and we need someone to find it. Something's been stolen, and we need a hero to retrieve it.

The gospel of Jesus Christ is a tale of true heroism. Paradise was stolen when the jealous serpent snaked his way into Adam's and Eve's thought life. They lost something much more precious than a gold heart locket. They lost the innocence of their hearts. They lost their garden. They lost their freedom. They lost heaven on earth. They lost their uninterrupted life with God.

Adam and Eve were responsible for their own errors just as we are. But their fall explains why we're all damsels in distress. We're vulnerable maidens. We've been violated. The devil is a cheap, two-bit mugger. He's a jealous, ruthless thief who lives in total darkness but who'll try to rob us blind in broad daylight. He'll snatch the most precious things of our hearts, not because he finds them valuable, but just so our hearts will bleed.

What part of paradise has the mugger stolen from you? A marriage? A dream? A reputation?

What's missing in your life that once was close to your heart? Do you long to laugh again? Maybe he's stolen your joy. Do you long to sleep again? Maybe he's pickpocketed your peace. Do you long to risk intimacy? Maybe he's stolen your confidence.

I can guess how you feel. Violated—because you know you've been attacked. Ashamed—because you never should have given the thief the opportunity. Helpless—because you know you can't get your treasures back by yourself. If that's how you feel, I know just what you need.

A true hero.

When Adam and Eve fell, a hero arose. Before Eve had swallowed the first bite of death, our hero made plans to swallow up death's bite. When God saw the crime in Eden, He made a decision: never to rest until the treasure was restored. When He witnessed the theft, He made a promise to His bride: "I will repay you for the years the locusts have eaten" (Joel 2:25).

That's why Jesus came. "The Son of Man came to seek and to save what was lost" (Luke 19:10). "The thief comes only to steal and kill and destroy; I have come that they may have life, and have it to the full" (John 10:10).

Jesus the hero—He does what you can't do for yourself. Jesus the hero—He saves the perishing. Jesus the hero—He returns stolen goods to their rightful owners.

A remarkable saint in my church died two weeks ago. Judy was beautiful inside and out. Some might remember how cancer cut her life short. But most will remember how long she lived after the diagnosis: seventeen years. Judy mystified the doctors with her perseverance. She blessed her friends with her witness. Most mortals in her condition couldn't have lived as she did.

When I had the privilege of addressing her family and friends at Judy's memorial service, I read a passage that I often read at funerals. But this time a word leaped out at me as if I'd never seen it before. "When the perishable has been clothed with the imperishable…the saying that is written will come true: 'Death has been swallowed up in victory.'…Thanks be to God! He *gives* us the victory through our Lord Jesus Christ" (1 Corinthians 15:54, 57, italics mine).

Note: He *gives* us the victory.

Maybe you've never noticed this word either. Have you pondered how strangely the word fits the verse? We talk often about living the victorious Christian life. But think about it. How can a victory be a gift?

I've always thought of victory as an accomplishment. If an athlete strives, trains hard, and performs well on game day, he wins. If he is out of shape or chokes when the pressure is on, he loses. Championships are won through hard work, athletic prowess, and a few good breaks. But victories are not gifts.

Similarly, most Christians think of spiritual victory as a sort of accomplishment. Run hard, keep one step in front of the devil, pray an hour each day, and memorize scripture every week; we call it living the victorious Christian life. But if you get down in the dumps one day, choke on your own prayers, and cry in your pillow, we call it living a defeated life.

Spiritual accomplishment could be the measuring stick of Christian victory except for that strangely inserted word *gives*. It violates our whole concept of winning. I ask again: How can victory be a gift?

As I pondered the question, I first thought of myself as the third-string water boy on the Super Bowl championship team. I figured Jesus to be the star quarterback who wins the game with several phenomenal touchdown passes. I don't do much, but because I'm on His team, I get to celebrate the victory too.

But that metaphor falls short. The Scripture's picture of victory is more personal. The Bible tells me that *I* am more than a conqueror. Judy was an individual champion, not just a team participant.

Judy was more like a wrestler who struggled against a formidable foe. Put yourself in her place. For most of the match you have the winning edge, but you can't seem to get your opponent permanently pinned. Then, toward the end of the match, the foe exerts a final strong move against you and puts you on your back. The referee raises his hand, ready to slap the mat and call the match.

But, imagine it: An Olympic, heavyweight wrestler leaps from the bleachers onto the mat and joins the fray. He picks you and your opponent off the mat, flips you both, puts you on top, and presses your foe's shoulders against the floor. The referee excitedly slaps his hand to the floor and shouts, "Pinned!" Quickly he hoists your hand in the air and announces you the champion.

Your opponent protests, of course. "It isn't fair," he cries. "You're *giving* him the victory. I was about to win. You turned everything upside down."

Everyone is surprised at the turn of events except you. You know why the Olympian came down to help you when all seemed lost. You sneak a glance at the hero and wink. After all, he's your Husband. Then you look at the ref. You don't need to say much. He smiles at you, and you smile back while you whisper, "I'm sure glad you were the referee. Nobody else would have called it like that, Dad."

That's when victory is a gift.

"Death has been swallowed up in victory." It suddenly made sense. At the very moment the devil seemed to have Judy pinned, a hero emerged. Her heavenly Husband pinned the foe. Her heavenly Father raised her hand high. "Thanks be to God! He gives us the victory through our Lord Jesus Christ."

When you're wrestling, remember: "our struggle is not against flesh and blood, but against the rulers, against the authorities, against the powers of this dark world and against the spiritual forces of evil in the heavenly realms" (Ephesians 6:12). You should certainly pray, stay in the Word, and wear the full armor of God. But know this: Spiritual victory is not something you earn—it is something you accept. The Christian life is not so much about what you have done—it's about what Christ has done. It's not so much about how strong you are—it's about how strong God is.

*E*lizabeth had a hero on the subway. He sacrificed his seat on her behalf. He chased down the bad guy, took back the stolen heart locket, and restored the gold to its rightful owner.

But I didn't mention the conclusion to this true story. It's the best part. A few months later he gave her some more gold. It was a ring. Elizabeth's hero became her husband.

You have a hero for life's journey. Don't be surprised to have precious things snatched from you. "In this world you will have trouble," Jesus said. The serpent is still slithering. The devil is still mugging. "But take heart! I have overcome the world" (John 16:33). Jesus gave up His heavenly seat, chased down the devil, took back your stolen heart, and offered you life again.

Jesus is a superhero. But unlike Bond or Batman, the Son of God did not whisk in for an amazing rescue and then disappear. Instead, when Jesus offered you back your stolen goods, He also offered a much greater gift. He offered Himself. He offered His own Spirit whom He called the Advocate. He offered Himself to stay by your side, ready to defend you against the enemy at all times.

Everyone needs a hero. Be glad you have an eternal hero in Jesus.

More than that, be glad your hero is also your Husband.

CHAPTER NINE

BETROTHED

"I will come back and take you to be with me."
John 14:3

ere's a riddle: When can an unmarried woman have a husband who wants a divorce? Answer: when she is betrothed.

Consider the mother of Jesus. When the Messiah was in Mary's womb, she wasn't married. That's why her pregnancy was so scandalous. There had been no wedding, but Matthew tells us: "Joseph her husband...had in mind to divorce her quietly" (Matthew 1:19).

In Western culture a man proposes to a woman. If she says yes, the man might give her an engagement ring. The couple might get married in a week, or they might wait two years. Either way, if they have a little tiff, she's welcome to throw the ring across the room at him, stick out her tongue, and storm out the door. Wedding's off. Maybe next week the wedding will be on again. Up and down, on and off—so goes the modern-day engagement.

But a Jewish couple in Jesus' day never would have imagined such a romantic roller-coaster ride. The process of marriage was clear, and no one stepped out of its healthy bounds. Once a groom's family had secured the consent of a bride, a betrothal agreement was written. The formal, signed document spelled out the conditions of betrothal. It was much more than an engagement. The groom offered much more than a ring. Often the groom's family gave a sizable sum of money or goods to the bride's family.

Once betrothed, the man and woman were permanently united and were properly called husband and wife. The formal betrothal agreement could not be undone without a divorce. But, unlike our promiscuous culture, the betrothed husband and wife would have no sexual union until their official marriage a year later.

During the year-long betrothal, the groom went back to his father's house to prepare a new home for his bride. The betrothed man might build an annex or upper room. If he had plenty of money and real estate, he might build an entirely new house. Whatever he built, he constructed it with care and passion. He was preparing a place for his beloved.

Once the new home was prepared, the groom's father inspected it. Satisfied that things were in order and convinced the time was right, the father sent the groom to get his bride. With loud, jubilant voices, the news stretched across the bride's village: "The bridegroom is coming!" The bride, prepared for her groom, met him amid song and dance. The couple was escorted through the village with light. Well-wishers looked through open windows and hollered out blessings.

Jewish families in those days really knew how to throw a party, especially at a wedding.

A Hebrew family went all out for the sake of festivity. First, the guests banqueted together at a scrumptious marriage feast. Then after the marriage ceremony, family and friends filled the groom's home with laughter, song, and dance for seven days. The bride and groom were prince and princess for a week. The great marriage party was something every betrothed couple looked forward to.

That's not to say that the year of betrothal wasn't beautiful in its own way. It was. Betrothed couples could have a lot of fun preparing for marriage. They could share their lives deeply. But there were limits to their intimacy. They belonged to each other, but they didn't wake up daily face to face.

Totally committed but not totally united. Plenty to celebrate but still preparing for the real party. Already husband and wife but not yet married. That's the picture of betrothal.

And that's the beautiful picture of a Christian on earth.

God the Father sent His Spirit into the world to seek a match for His only Son. He noticed you. It was love at first sight. His affection fell upon you. He wooed you, enticed you, allured you. He paid an enormous bride price at a place called Golgotha. And when you consented to His betrothal agreement, you became His bride—His betrothed.

The betrothal agreement was sealed by the witness of His Spirit. Nothing can break it. You're His. He is yours. Rightly you can be called the wife of this heavenly Husband. All the benefits of the marriage relationship are promised to you.

But something better awaits. You've plenty to celebrate during your betrothal, but the real wedding party is yet to come.

*H*aven't you noticed that even life's best moments are at least slightly tarnished? Don't you have a sense that no matter how good it gets, it's not quite good enough? Even my highest moments of earthly bliss—like the birth of my little boy—are at least slightly tainted by worldly concern. When Bennett poked his head into the world in the wee morning hours after my champion wife had labored all day, I held him first and wept for joy. What moment equals the bliss of holding your own newborn? But the doctors didn't let me hold him very long. They were concerned about a little chirp in his cry and hustled him into the nursery where they could monitor his breathing. It proved to be no problem, but it did serve as a reminder that earth's best moments are still not heaven.

And I remember my wedding. It was grand—mostly. But one groomsman left in the middle of the service for fear of fainting. At the reception the video recorder's battery expired, so we have no film of our wedding reception. A guest lingered too long at the shrimp bowl, and the shrimp ran out. A young woman felt compelled to hang around my bride and me throughout the reception until she was in our every picture and on our every nerve.

Even our best parties come up short.

Do you ever wonder what's going to make heaven's party so great? Part of the answer is tucked away in Jesus' parable on the subject. "At that time," He began, "the kingdom of heaven will be like ten virgins who took their lamps and went out to meet the bridegroom" (Matthew 25:1).

In Jesus' time bridesmaids not only helped prepare the bride. On the day of the wedding they also would rush out to meet the bridegroom. With light, song, and dance, they welcomed the groom and then escorted the couple through the village to the groom's newly prepared home. Jesus' parable describes five of the bridesmaids as foolish because they took no oil to refuel their lights. These lights were not little flickering candles but mighty torches—long sticks with oil-saturated cloths at the end. When the bridesmaids heard the bridegroom was on his way, they quickly set flame to their torches and held them high.

I like to imagine the bridegroom standing on a distant hill in the dark, Judean night air. I envision him looking across the valley to the hill whose side is dotted with the village of his betrothed. It is midnight. All is quiet, tranquil, and dark. But even from a distance he sees the light of ten torches flooding his bride's courtyard. He points, smiles, and shouts, "There's my bride—I see her light. Let me go get her!"

I wonder if Jesus will come back like that. Standing on the crest of the universe, He peers at the visited planet. There, amid the spiritual darkness, the Messiah sees the torches of the saints lifted high. The heavenly Bridegroom points, smiles, and shouts, "There's My bride—her light is still shining. Let Me go get her!"

The picture makes me pause to ponder: When the heavenly Bridegroom looks across the span of humanity, will He see my light shining brightly?

Sadly, the foolish bridesmaids' torches hastily grew dim. They would have lasted only about fifteen minutes—the amount of time such a torch could endure before flickering, fading, and expiring. With no oil to fuel their flames, the five panic-stricken, foolish bridesmaids begged the others for some of their oil.

"No," the wise bridesmaids replied, "there may not be enough for both us and you." The wise attendants weren't stingy or spiteful. Rather, they understood that if they shared half their oil with the foolish women, soon everyone would run out of oil. No one would have enough fuel to light the night sky when the bridegroom arrived. No one would have light left to escort the bridegroom and bride through town.

Dry torches don't burn. No oil—no flame. No flame—no light.

Dry religion doesn't burn. No oil of the Holy Spirit—no inward flame. No inward flame—no light unto the world.

The foolish bridesmaids left in desperation to buy some oil. "But while they were on their way to buy the oil," the parable continues, "the bridegroom arrived. The virgins who were ready went in with him to the wedding banquet. And the door was shut. Later the others also came. 'Sir! Sir!' they said. 'Open the door for us!' But he replied, 'I tell you the truth, I don't know you'" (Matthew 25:10–12).

Sometimes we get a big dose of heaven on earth. But it seems like every time life becomes a heavenly party, somebody tries to crash the door. Every time your wick burns brightly, someone wants to take your oil.

Think about it. You can have

...worship so beautiful that everyone hears the brush of angels' wings, but somebody doesn't like the color of the communion tablecloth;

...a sermon so stirring that scores repent, but somebody's face is sour because she's going to be late to lunch;

...fellowship so genuine that broken hearts are mended, but somebody is irked because the beans at the fellowship dinner are too mushy;

...prayer so powerful that a cancer disappears, but somebody's aghast because the meeting seemed too charismatic;

...compassion so sweet that the homeless in your town finally find a home, but somebody's critical because the church isn't charismatic enough.

Every time God sends a parade on earth, the devil sends some dark cloud to rain on it. Every time a Christian's lamp gets really bright, the devil sends some dried-up torch to try to diminish it. Every time the heavenly party on earth gets lively, the devil sends some cold wick to crash it.

Do you know what's going to make the heavenly wedding party so spectacular? No party poopers.

Imagine it. No dried-up torches—only heaven's pure light. No cold religion—just pure praise. No critical spirits—just real joy. No dead wicks—just live wires.

Heaven's party will have no party poopers. No darkness will be allowed.

It won't be because the bridesmaids inside are stingy or spiteful. It will be because the party must be pure celebration. When you celebrate in heaven, no one will look down on you. They'll dance beside you. When you feast in the reception hall of the King of kings, the shrimp will never run out. The music will not stop. And you'll never feel like a fool for praising Him.

*L*ife may be tough for you right now. I'm not sure what storm is attempting to douse your parade. Your husband might have left you without an explanation. Your company might have left you without a job. Your best friend might have left you without a reputation. It hurts. But it no longer surprises me. It just proves that the real wedding party has not yet begun.

So get ready. If you have given your heart to Christ, you are His betrothed. That means already but not yet. You're already His, but you're not yet living in your new home. It means He's already your Husband, but the real marriage awaits. It means as good as it might get here, the best is yet to come.

Meanwhile, keep your own oil jar filled. Celebrate as brightly as you can. But remember, the Bridegroom's coming back for His betrothed:

"If I go and prepare a place for you, I will come back and take you to be with me that you also may be where I am" (John 14:3).

CHAPTER TEN

JUST MARRIED

Like newborn babies, crave pure spiritual milk.
1 Peter 2:2

*N*ewlyweds are naive. I'm sure Anne and I were more naive than most.

I married a North Carolina girl whose Christian heritage and delicate, southern upbringing had kept her cleaner than a spring lamb. Sneaking a search for crayfish in Silas Creek ranked among her most radical childhood sins. In fact, when she and her preschool friends played dress-up, she pretended to be the minister's wife. By first grade she had already started witnessing to her friends. The first time a teenage date made a pass at her, she blackened his eye with her elbow.

Thankfully, when I married Anne, she was still sweeter than her mother's Christmas coffee cake. But she was a bit naive. When we found the crass license plates that a few of my less innocent groomsmen had planted in our honeymoon luggage as a prank, my new wife didn't even catch their off-color messages. When we walked a portion of New Orleans's Bourbon Street on the way back from the restaurant to our French Quarter honeymoon hotel, it was her eyes that were bulging out. In fact, having never before seen someone drunk in a gutter, she desperately tried to persuade me to perform CPR on a passed-out partyer.

My wife was truly naive in the ways of the world.

I, on the other hand, was truly naive in the ways of refinement. Anne had recently won a week-long honeymoon trip for two to New Orleans as a contestant on *The Price Is Right*. (Yeah, she kissed Bob Barker and won about $20,000 worth of stuff including the showcase, and, no, I didn't marry her purely for her game-show dowry.) Since I was the youngest of three rowdy boys, my middle-class parents never risked taking me to a nice hotel. They claim we once went to a posh ski resort, but I don't remember going, and I've never seen any pictures to prove I was there. I once toured the whole country with two six-foot-two-inch college buddies in one Honda Prelude, but our idea of posh was a campground with potable water.

Nonetheless, I tried to act genteel and experienced when we arrived in our rented car at the French Quarter high-rise. I had never handed my keys to a valet parking service or had a man tote my bags, but I managed what I considered a suave demeanor. I sloughed off the momentary embarrassment when the bell captain gave me a silly grin and asked, "On your honeymoon?" Assuming it was our youthful looks alone that gave us away, I proudly led my bride to our room on the twenty-fourth floor. Once I figured out how to use the computer-card key, we crossed the threshold.

The Price Is Right had done us right. Our hotel room was a beautiful expanse of living space. As one who'd never stayed in a place that provided little shampoo bottles, I was especially impressed by the TV affixed to the bathroom wall. (Later, when anyone asked about our room, the bathroom TV was always the first thing I mentioned.)

My attempt to appear cultured went well until our return from dinner that first night. Whatever success at feigned sophistication I had accomplished thus far was totally blown as we reentered our room.

I began my customary ritual of shoving the computer card in and out of the door slot. After several failed attempts, we heard a frightening sound. Voices in our room! We double-checked the room number. It was ours all right. Finally I got the door unlocked. Boldly I entered. A quick, heroic canvass of the room revealed no intruder. But someone had turned on the radio! There were other signs of entry as well. Towels were out. Bed linens were altered. I placed an urgent call to the front desk. As I was describing the scene in our room, I noticed the bedside tables and thought, *How strange that a thief would leave mints for us.*

It was too late to hang up the phone and save face. I just had to swallow hard and endure the muffled laughs of the front-desk clerk as he assured me it was all part of their nightly turndown service.

Naive? I admit it. If you've been single all your life, lived with bunches of male don't-mind-if-mold-grows-in-the-tub slobs, and spent your only nights out at Motel 6, it's hard to know how to act in a French Quarter high-rise with a TV in your bathroom, mints on the bedstand, and a beautiful woman in your bed.

We were easily pegged. All honeymooning couples are easy to spot.

And so are "honeymooning" Christians.

When a sinner discovers grace and says "I do" to the Giver of that wondrous mercy, the new believer grows starry eyed over his new love. I'm not scorning the freshly regenerated soul. Beholding the miracle of new birth is my greatest delight. But perhaps we should consider tagging the new Christian with a "Just Married" sign. Or maybe we should tie a few tin cans to the spiritual newborn's ankles to give fair warning to the unsuspecting public. New Christians are like spiritual honeymooners. They hardly know what to do with themselves.

Consider the euphoric joy that makes newlyweds feel like all their problems have disappeared forever. Newlyweds blush a lot, giggle a lot, and daydream a lot. They can't understand why everyone else isn't so happy. And when they encounter an unhappy, unmarried person, the honeymooner secretly thinks, *You poor, pathetic, lonely fool. You need to get married like I just did.*

Some "spiritual newlyweds" experience an even more wonderful euphoria. Not just new Christians but also seasoned Christians who have a fresh encounter in the Spirit become giddy in the wonder of God's love. It's an exciting time of passionate growth in God. Spiritual honeymooners are on fire for God!

But they aren't always sensitive to others.

The spiritual newlywed can't understand why Deacon Doubleduty wants to spend an evening with his family instead of attending the youth lock-in. The on-fire believer can't fathom why Brother Glumface and Sister Slumpneck don't want to clap and sing. And sometimes the spiritual honeymooner is so busy trying to get less-renewed church friends to have his same fresh-fire experience that he becomes blind to their genuine pain.

*J*ust Married" couples are also naive about the difficulties ahead. I always try to counsel the premarital couple carefully about the battles before them. They smile, nod their heads, mutter some acknowledgment that they know marriage isn't easy, and then giggle again. It's tough to counteract the societal norm that if you want to be happy, all you have to do is fall in love and get married.

Honeymooners don't realize that the whole fallen world is geared to destroy their marriage. They can be brainwashed by the TV, distracted by their work, stressed by their finances, and misled by their lost friends. And when they wake up one day and discover that marriage hasn't solved all their problems, they're prone to get a double dose of reality and discouragement. Sometimes, like Elijah after Mount Carmel, we face our greatest despair on the heels of our greatest celebration.

Likewise, blissfully "Just Married" Christians are not yet aware of the spiritual battles ahead. Jesus warned His disciples, "In this world you will have trouble" (John 16:33). He cautioned them, "I am sending you out like sheep among wolves. Therefore be as shrewd as snakes and as innocent as doves" (Matthew 10:16).

When you give your hand to the heavenly Groom and openly speak your vows, you also gain a mortal foe who hates your holy Husband and therefore hates you. This diabolic enemy has one hellish goal: to destroy your marriage made in heaven. While you are adorned with the beautiful jewels of grace and divine affection, do not forget also to don your spiritual armor each day of your new life. The honeymoon joy is real—but so is the battle ahead.

*N*ewlyweds are naive. Naive about others' pain. Naive about obstacles ahead. But mostly—and most wonderfully—they are naive about the wonders set before them.

Amid their giggling, starry-eyed honeymoon delight, "Just Married" couples can't even imagine a better day. What could be better than new love? What could be more delightful than honeymoon bubble baths and candlelight room service? What could be more fulfilling than to have a new beginning with no old wounds to mend?

Newlyweds can hardly imagine anything better than a honeymoon.

But ask the few lifelong partners who have chosen to walk the road less traveled, and they'll tell you of something greater. Ask the few who have chosen to walk the path of true commitment. Real love. God's kind of selfless love. Ask them if there is something better than a honeymoon. Ask a wife who's learned the love that is not self-seeking. Ask a husband who's learned to lay his life down for his beloved. Ask them. They can tell you

...that shared memories settle into layers of depth that, over time, build mountains of strength;

...that there is an ecstasy in seeing your baby's first smile that unspeakably exceeds the pleasure of the honeymoon act that conceived the child;

...that shared pain, though unwelcome at the time of trouble, refines love like a goldsmith's fire and that holding your husband's hand while he selects his mother's casket, or praying

together until a wayward teenage child comes home can build a fellowship of suffering more intimate than any wedding night could ever offer;

...that shared triumphs—celebrations of hurdles you've overcome together—carry a far deeper joy than honeymoon hot-tub bubbles ever can;

...that when you look into the eyes of someone who loves you more today, even though she's had many years to see your deepest defects, it greatly surpasses the infatuation of untested newlyweds.

And there is a kindred promise for every freshly infatuated Christian. Just ask Peter. Newlywed Peter. Ask impetuous, exuberant, naive Peter.

When he fell in love with the Groom, this newlywed Christian tried to walk on water. But his tiptoe through high tide wasn't rooted in storm-tested, seasoned faith. It was a wonderful, brief, honeymoon stroll...until naive Peter took his eyes off the Groom and the turbulent sea overwhelmed him.

Oh, Peter. Naive, speak-now-and-think-later Peter. When his princely Groom spoke of coming persecution, Peter exclaimed, "Even if all fall away on account of you, I never will" (Matthew 26:33). Naive, newlywed Peter really thought no fear could overtake him. When the cock crowed thrice, I wonder if he said to himself, *Uh-oh. Honeymoon's over.*

Oh, Peter. Naive, I-can-save-the-world Peter. When the soldiers came to take Peter's Beloved away, the honeymooning disciple hacked off servant Malchus's ear. It was a noble, passionate act from a "Just Married" Christian. "Peter, dear Peter," Jesus may have said as He healed the servant's severed ear, "Do you not see the futility of this strike? This man already has no ears to hear."

But Peter's impetuous, naive faith grew. Oh, how it grew. He chose to walk the road of lasting, lavish love. It was Peter who preached the Pentecost sermon (Acts 2:14). It was Peter who prophesied to the high priest (Acts 4:6–8) and walked with an angel past prison guards (Acts 12:8–10). It was Peter who commanded Tabitha to arise from the dead (Acts 9:40).

If anyone understood how great life with the Groom can grow, Peter did. His epistles more than any others exhort believers to "rejoice [when they] participate in the sufferings of Christ" (1 Peter 4:13) and to hold to the "enduring word of God" (1 Peter 1:23). Interestingly, the once-naive Peter even urges young men to "be submissive to those who are older" (1 Peter 5:5).

And no one could have more aptly penned this admonition to newlywed Christians: "Like newborn babies, crave pure spiritual milk, so that by it you may grow up in your salvation, now that you have tasted that the Lord is good" (1 Peter 2:2–3).

*D*elight in your honeymoon, new Christian. Revel in your fresh touch of the Spirit, faithful disciple. But whatever taste of His grace you have experienced, keep drinking. Stay at the fountain of your nourishment.

You were not betrothed to this Husband for the mere thrill of a honeymoon. You accepted a proposal to walk and grow in love.

Ask any seasoned saint who has walked in that love. He or she can tell you

> ...*that there is a grandeur to God's grace that is not seen until the test of time has revealed the Groom's enduring faithfulness;*
>
> ...*that there is a fellowship of suffering with Christ that draws you into a spiritual intimacy far deeper than any marshmallow-roasting, campfire "Kum Ba Yah";*
>
> ...*that the Groom becomes altogether more heroic when you face the greatest battles of your life and you behold your Prince charging before you to the front line;*
>
> ...*that no matter how far you walk with God on earth, this life is a short-lived honeymoon preparing you for an eternity of anniversaries.*

I hope you weren't as naive as I was on my honeymoon. I hope you didn't mistake mints for mayhem. More importantly, I hope you never mistake temporary euphoria for enduring love.

If you are on your spiritual honeymoon, enjoy it. Burn brightly. But remember: As good as your honeymoon days with Christ may be, I can promise you more. There is an enduring glow of God's love that burns more brightly, more warmly, more wonderfully, than even the brightest honeymoon fire.

CHAPTER ELEVEN

TAKING HIS NAME

"Blessed is he who comes in the name of the Lord!"
Mark 11:9

My church's music minister has a common name, David Smith. But believe me, the man himself isn't common. He's one of a kind. You wouldn't believe some of the stuff that has happened to him.

One time he was with a group of strangers playing an "ice breaker" designed to help people get to know one another. Maybe you've played it before. Each player wears the name of a celebrity on his or her back. The object of the game is to find out what your celebrity name is. Contestants discover their names by asking simple questions of others who are playing the game. You can ask questions like: "Am I alive or dead?" and "Am I a movie star?"

David, in his normal gregarious manner, approached a couple he'd never seen before. With exaggerated gesture and overdone expression, he asked slowly, "Am I a man or a woman?"

"Wh-a-a-t?" the husband gasped as he drew closer to his wife.

Again David drew out his question with a silly expression, "Am I a man or a woman?"

When my outgoing musical friend watched the couple's faces contort a second time, he realized what he'd done. Swallowing hard, he stuttered, "You're not playing the game, are you?"

The couple withdrew even more. "What game?"

I'd like to have heard David wriggle his way out of that one. Maybe the lesson is don't play games with names. Names are really important. Our identity is all wrapped up in a name.

When Anne and I named our baby, I remembered that in biblical days names were often prophetic. Prayerfully we named him Matthew ("gift of God") Bennett ("blessing") Wright. We considered calling him Bennett Matthew Wright. But that order would have made his initials BMW. I didn't want my boy expecting a fulfillment of prophecy on his sixteenth birthday.

Peter was a man who lived up to his prophetic name. Originally his name was Simon, or "unstable." It seemed a fitting name for the impetuous disciple. Simon was a pretty shifty fellow. One day he claimed he would never forsake Jesus; the next day he claimed he'd never known Him. Despite Simon's shifting-sand character, Jesus saw substance in the man and wanted everyone to know about it. So the Lord decided to call him "Rock."

Since the meanings of names were readily understood in biblical times, it meant a lot for someone to get a new name. It was like receiving a whole new identity. Oftentimes when a life-changing event occurred in a person's life, he or she would get a new name. Abram became Abraham. Sarai became Sarah. Jacob became Israel. Saul became Paul.

People don't receive new names very often in our society. Spies use aliases, and federal witnesses are given new identities. But, generally speaking, people in our culture keep their names.

Only one group of people regularly gets new names: brides. Most women take a new last name when they marry, sometimes for better, sometimes for worse.

A man named George Fling married his sweetheart, whose name was Katherine Last. The local newspaper headline properly announced their wedding: *Last-Fling*. I hope their marriage lasted with no other flings.

Mr. and Mrs. Hugh Hogg's daughter married her beloved, whose name was Russell G. Hamm. Surely the town news editors could have found a better headline than they did: *Hogg and Hamm to Exchange Vows*.[1] Miss Hogg became Mrs. Hamm.

In another real-life wedding, Miss Wong became Mrs. Wright.

With all the romance, beauty, and misty eyes on a wedding day, we hardly consider the name that's changing. But, practically speaking, it may be the most dramatic change of all. It's quite bizarre, really—proceeding with one name, receding with another. On what other day can Hoggs become Hamms and Wongs become Wrights? It's a huge change for the woman. After the wedding-day excitement, the bride has a lot of paperwork ahead. She needs a new checkbook, driver's license, and social security card. She has to learn a new signature and develop a new introduction of herself.

As a man, it's hard for me to imagine what it's like to change your name midstream. Men talk a lot about "building a name" for themselves. That's the way of the independent American male. Marriage is just the opposite. It's not about making a name; it's about taking a name.

Of course, some women keep their maiden names after marriage. Some create a new, hyphenated name (although I doubt Miss Hogg would have gone for Mrs. Hogg-Hamm). Still, most brides enter the wedding chapel with the name of their birth and leave with the name of their husbands.

It can be risky for a woman to take another name. If the man's name falls under scandal, she shares the shame. If her husband's name becomes infamous, so does hers. It's a vulnerable step of trust to take someone else's name.

But it can also be a tremendous gift. A good name, made honorable through years of righteous standing in the community, is a unique wedding present. Marriage is the one place where you can gain a good name without earning it.

You can imagine the fairy tale: A humble woman from a meager upbringing marries a prince. On her wedding day she exchanges her common name for a royal name. The bride gets all the blessing of royalty with her new name: a noble reputation, prominence in society, credibility in the community. All that—for free! Actually a good name is one thing money can't purchase. A good name is either built or begotten, but it's never bought.

When a man shares his name with a woman in marriage, there's risk and reward for him too. A thoughtless wife can drag her husband's good name through the dirt. She can't ruin the name, but she sure can muddy it. On the other hand, a man who gives his name to a noble bride gains much. His name is multiplied. Wherever she goes, his good name goes. The lives that she touches, he touches.

*Y*ou see where we're going with this, don't you? When you are wed to Christ, incredible changes occur. The wonder of His love engulfs you. The promise of His presence lifts you. The vows He speaks secure you. This marriage to the Lord is so marvelous in all its many facets that perhaps you've missed one of the most staggering facts of all. The bride gets the Bridegroom's good name.

You walk down the aisle to Christ with an earthly name; you marry into a heavenly name. You come to the wedding with a name of flesh; you dance at the wedding banquet with a name of Spirit. You get an unbelievable gift: the name of the Prince of Peace, the name that is above every other name. You acquire the name of the Lord. You become a Christian, a "Christ-one." You take on the highest, most noble, most respected, most powerful name in the universe. It is the name unto which every knee will one day bow. It's not a name that you built. It's a name that Christ made for Himself by living a perfect life. He built the name. He bought you. You gained the name—for free.

God has always planned for His bride to share His name.

The LORD said to Moses, "Tell Aaron and his sons, 'This is how you are to bless the Israelites. Say to them:
"""The LORD bless you
  and keep you;
the LORD make his face shine upon you
  and be gracious to you;
the LORD turn his face toward you
  and give you peace.""'
"So they will put my name on the Israelites, and I will bless them."

Numbers 6:22–27 (emphasis added)

To give His name is to give His blessing: "Blessed is he who comes in the name of the Lord!" (Mark 11:9). It was Jesus' secret ingredient to all effective prayer: "the Father will give you whatever you ask *in my name*" (John 15:16, emphasis added).

There's unspeakable power in Jesus' name. But it's not a magic word to be used for tricks. It's an identity to be worn for life.

On one occasion some Jews were trying to cast out evil spirits using the name of Jesus. The sons of a chief priest tried to command a devil to flee "in the name of Jesus; whom Paul preaches." There was only one problem: The boys weren't wed to the Name. They didn't wear or bear the Name; they just wanted to use it. Big mistake. "One day the evil spirit answered them, 'Jesus I know, and I know about Paul, but who are you?' Then the man who had the evil spirit jumped on them and overpowered them all. He gave them such a beating that they ran out of the house naked and bleeding" (Acts 19:13, 15–16).

When a woman marries, she doesn't merely use her husband's name. She becomes it.

*O*ne winter's night in North Korea, Richard Manning and Ray Brennan huddled inside a bunker a hundred yards behind enemy lines. It was January 1952. Snow was falling on the two marines who happened to be best friends. They were preparing to crawl through enemy territory and sweep the trail for mines so their troops could move forward in assault at dawn. Here's how Richard described what happened next:

We were passing a chocolate bar back and forth. Ray took the last bite when a grenade lobbed by an undetected North Korean landed squarely in the center of the bunker. Ray was the first one to spot it. Almost nonchalantly he flipped the candy wrapper aside and fell on the grenade. It detonated instantly. His stomach smothered the explosion. I was completely unharmed, untouched. He looked up at me, winked, and rolled over dead.[2]

Eight years later Richard was taking his vows to become a Franciscan priest. For years, the Franciscans had required a priest to change his name to another saint's name as a symbol of his new identity. But the year Richard took his vows the Catholic Church decided to let priests choose their own first names. That's how Richard Manning became Brennan Manning, the well-known author.

It made sense, of course. If you're going to take someone else's name, you want to take the name of the one who loves you most. So Richard exchanged his name for the name of the one who died for him. Now, everywhere Manning goes, Brennan's name goes also. If anyone asks Brennan Manning where he got his name, he can tell them plainly, "From the man who saved my life."

Two thousand years ago another explosive detonated—not in a bunker in North Korea but outside Jerusalem on a hill called Calvary. It was more like a nuclear bomb than a grenade. The wrath should have killed you and me. Instead, the entire destructive force was absorbed by one Man. The man's name was Yeshua, which means simply, "the Lord saves."

Once wed to Christ, you get to take the name of the One who loves you most. And, if anyone asks you where you got your name, you can say plainly, "From the One who saved my life."

One day soon there's going to be a huge wedding party in a heavenly city. We may not know each other's names right now, but there won't be any need to play name-guessing ice breakers when we meet in heaven. "The throne of God and of the Lamb will be in the city, and his servants will serve him. They will see his face, *and his name will be on their foreheads*" (Revelation 22:3–4, emphasis added).

If I never get a chance to meet you on earth, I'll look forward to seeing you at the party where everyone has a built-in name tag. Until then, "whatever you do, whether in word or deed, do it all *in the name of the Lord Jesus,* giving thanks to God the Father through him" (Colossians 3:17, emphasis added).

CHAPTER TWELVE

KNOWING HIM

Now Samuel did not yet know the LORD.
1 Samuel 3:7

"Adam knew Eve."

Intriguing words, aren't they? *"Adam knew Eve."* The words initiate the fourth chapter of Genesis in the King James Version. But Adam and Eve had been on earth since Genesis chapter 1. A lot had happened in those chapters.

Initially they had no shame. I'm sure they took a good, long look at each other. They ate together and walked together in the garden. They probably worked some and played some together. They beheld the best in one another. They also saw the worst. They ate of the same rotten fruit. They wore clothes woven of the same fig fabric. They walked silently in the same direction out of Eden. They glanced back at the same flashing cherubim's sword.

After all that wouldn't you say Adam and Eve knew each other pretty well? Yet not until chapter 4 does the Bible finally say, "Adam *knew* Eve."

I used to think it was a euphemism—a polite way to talk about a sensitive subject. Nice Christians don't talk openly about sex. So we say things like "they went to bed" or "they slept together." Assuming the Hebrews were similarly squeamish about the subject, I figured the biblical writers skirted it by using carefully chosen words: "Adam knew Eve."

But why would God, who authored the words, be embarrassed about human sexuality? He proudly created the whole beautiful process. He deliberately and wonderfully fashioned us as sexual creatures—male and female. Our sexuality is our most fundamental feature. It's the first thing anyone is interested in. If you are a female, the first words you heard on earth were, "It's a girl!" Later, when you grew and matured physically, young men said the same thing of you again: "It's a girl, it's a girl!" God designed us as sexual beings on purpose. The Lord Almighty couldn't be squeamish about sex— He invented it.

"Adam knew Eve." It is no euphemism but a profound description of sexual union as the Lord designed it. It is a metaphor describing the deepest form of human sharing. It is the most vulnerable of earthly moments. It is the time when the fig leaves come off—when secrets are revealed. It is risky self-disclosure. Bare, unguarded revelation.

The Hebrew word for "to know" is used to describe other sexual relationships like Cain's marriage consummation (Genesis 4:17) and the virginity of Jephthah's daughter (Judges 11:39). But the same word also is used more than a thousand times in the Bible to describe mental or emotional knowledge of someone. It all makes me wonder: If the Bible calls a man's most intimate experience of his wife "knowing" her, what might God mean when He repeatedly admonishes us to "know the Lord"?

The answer is in the Hebrew bridal chamber.

The ancient Jewish wedding, much like today, was intensely public. The relationship began with a written betrothal agreement that was drawn up by the authorities, witnessed by others, and paid by the bridegroom. A marriage contract was then executed "according to the laws of Moses and of Israel." After the woman's consent, the document required the signatures of two witnesses. Everything was public.

In the evening of the day fixed for the marriage, the bridegroom and his friends proceeded openly through the village to the bride's house. Usually the bridegroom escorted the bride back to his parents' home for a big feast. The bridal party celebrated the procession with music, song, and dance as their lamps torched up the night sky. Well-wishing villagers shouted and applauded from their open windows.

Scores of relatives and friends attended the marriage feast. Parents and friends participated together in a public ceremony of blessing the couple. The marriage contract was read aloud for all to hear. After the marriage ceremony, a week-long party ensued. A Jewish wedding was a gala event for the entire community. A grand, open celebration.

The whole Jewish wedding was unabashedly public except for one element: the bridal chamber. After the marriage contract was read and public blessings were showered, the friend of the bridegroom escorted the couple to a private room. It was a secret space prepared exclusively for the groom and his bride. No one else entered the bridal chamber. There, like a whisper amidst shouts, the groom and bride were finally, completely, alone. For the first time, the bride lifted her veil. For the first time, she did what no proper Jewish woman would do in public: She let down her hair. And for the first time, the bride *knew* her husband.

For all its public fanfare, the real moment of marriage was hidden in the bridal chamber. Keep all the rest of the wedding festivities, but exclude the bridal chamber, and you've missed marriage. The bridal chamber made it more than a great, festive event. The bridal chamber made it a union.

Because I'm a pastor, my wife and I are, unavoidably, public people. We can enjoy a Sunday school social as much as anybody. In fact, my wife is usually the life of the party. As public people, we regularly graze at wedding reception tables and hug mourners beside gravestones. We attend a lot of public gatherings. We enjoy a whole range of "goof off" activities as well. But it's not the parties, the receptions, or the wakes that make us a married couple. It's the bedroom. Without the bedroom, we are good buddies, close companions, even committed partners—but not husband and wife.

It's daring to consider, but ponder it. If you are betrothed to Christ, the heavenly Bridegroom longs for the marriage's consummation. The infinite, eternal Creator of the universe wants to be as intimate with you as a bridegroom with his bride on their wedding night. The invitation to "know the Lord" is not, of course, sexual. It is spiritual. But perhaps you'll never understand the depth of God's love for you nor the heavenly intimacy available to you until you dare to meet Jesus in the bridal chamber of your heart.

Remember Jesus' puzzling, incisive words: "Many will say to me on that day, 'Lord, Lord, did we not prophesy in your name, and in your name drive out demons and perform many miracles?' Then I will tell them plainly, 'I never knew you. Away from me, you evildoers!'" (Matthew 7:22–23).

It's plain enough. Christ wants much more than your public, religious activities. The Lord wants to know you.

*I*t is possible to be quite busy in the church but unwed to the Lord. To pledge yourself to religious service but not know the God you serve. To talk about Him, teach about Him, even tell others about Him, but have no authentic intimacy with Him.

Consider Samuel's story.

One night as he lay sleeping, Samuel heard a voice calling him. He ran to Eli and said, "Here I am; you called me."

But Eli said, "I did not call; go back and lie down."

The voice came a second time, "Samuel!"

The boy ran to Eli again. Same answer. "Go back to bed, boy."

But the third time around, "Eli realized that the LORD was calling the boy. So Eli told Samuel, 'Go and lie down, and if he calls you, say, "Speak, LORD, for your servant is listening"'" (1 Samuel 3:4–9).

Imagine it. Three times he heard the direct, audible voice of God. And three times the boy missed it. The only reason he finally caught on was because the priest gave him specific instructions about what to do. Do you marvel at how persevering God is? At how much He wants to be heard?

The Bible gives us a clear explanation of Samuel's spiritual deafness. In the middle of the narrative, almost parenthetically, we're told: "Now Samuel did not yet know the LORD" (verse 7).

Didn't know the Lord yet? Wait a minute. This is the boy who was the product of his mother's weeping prayers. His name meant *"God answers prayer."* This is the lad who was dedicated to the Lord from the time he was weaned. Samuel "was ministering before the LORD—a boy wearing a linen ephod" (1 Samuel 2:18). The Bible clearly states that Samuel grew in "stature and in favor with the LORD and with men" (1 Samuel 2:26). By the time of his three-strikes-you-ought-to-be-out encounter with God's call, Samuel was at least twelve years old, perhaps older. The Bible says affectionately that he "grew up in the presence of the LORD" (1 Samuel 2:21).

How much more religious can you get? Samuel was born because of a miraculous conception. He was dedicated to the Lord as an infant. He ministered in the temple as a youth. He was the priest's best helper. He grew up in the presence of the Lord.

But he didn't know God.

It *is* possible. You can be born in a Christian home, be baptized, be miraculously healed of a childhood disease, sing solos in the children's choir, play Mary in the Christmas drama, be president of Pioneer Club, graduate from confirmation class, make honor roll at a Christian college, deliver daily meals to shut-ins, memorize the whole New Testament, teach the "Tweenagers" Sunday school class, be ordained, preach a rousing sermon, eulogize a dead saint, moderate the deacon board—and not know the Lord.

God never wanted His people to serve Him without knowing Him. The writer of Hebrews, echoing Jeremiah, explains.

If there had been nothing wrong with that first covenant, no place would have been sought for another. But God found fault with the people and said:

"The time is coming, declares the Lord,

when I will make a new covenant....

It will not be like the covenant

I made with their forefathers....

I will put my laws in their minds

and write them on their hearts.

I will be their God,

and they will be my people.

No longer will a man teach his neighbor,

or a man his brother, saying, 'Know the Lord,'

because they will all know me,

from the least of them to the greatest."

(Hebrews 8:7–11)

The Christian life is not outward conformity to rules—it is God's life in us. Real knowledge of God comes only when the Lord puts His truth *in* us. To know God is to receive Him. We must learn to yield to the Groom's gracious embrace. We must discover how to welcome His holy entrance into our hearts.

The bridal chamber is a place for union. Strongly, gently, unreservedly, a husband makes inward connection with his wife. Warmly, beautifully, vulnerably, she receives her husband's presence.

Human sexual intimacy requires two essentials: unguarded abandon and permanent commitment. A bride can't hide herself and be known by her husband. She can't be united with him while keeping him distant. With trust and joy, she must relinquish herself into his hands. At the same time, the consummation must be seated in total, lifetime commitment. Sex without marriage is only a shallow, obscene imitation of what it was designed to be.

*H*ow can we know God? As a pastor, I hear such questions as these all the time: "How can I experience more of God's love?" "What steps must I take to find true peace?" "What must I do to be baptized in the Holy Spirit?"

Spiritual intimacy with the heavenly Bridegroom is like earthly intimacy between a devoted husband and wife. It is more a result of right passion than right technique. Two things are needful for intimate knowledge of God: our unguarded abandon and our permanent commitment.

God wants more people who will lose sight of themselves long enough to be overwhelmed by the sight of God. The Messiah longs for more men and women who will throw caution to the wind and relinquish themselves unto the Lord. Jesus wants more who will jump out of the boat despite the wind and waves, more who will pour out their perfume despite its great cost.

At the same time, this Bridegroom demands total, permanent commitment. God will not be mocked. Nor will He be used. When the woman with the issue of blood touched Jesus' garment, the Messiah refused to travel on until He established a relationship with her. When Simon the magician tried to buy the ability to impart the Holy Spirit, he received nothing but admonition. Holy, intimate experiences of God are not for spiritual thrill seekers unprepared to walk with Him. Intimacy requires covenant.

You've spoken your vows. You've taken His name. Now it is time to slip away. The bridal chamber awaits. It might be your prayer closet, or it might be a pew seat. It might be under a preacher's powerful anointing or under a soft silence.

When you go there, don't be so concerned with the technique of your prayer or the structure of your devotion. Just express the passion of your love to God…and listen to hear the heartbeat of His. Please don't be scared to give all of yourself to Him. He's pure love. You can close the door on the world clamoring for your attention. Go ahead, lift your veil. Let down your hair. Show Him everything. Hold nothing back.

He really wants to know you. And, oh, how He wants to be known.

CHAPTER THIRTEEN

SWEET SOMETHINGS IN YOUR EAR

And after the fire came a gentle whisper.
1 Kings 19:12

*D*rill sergeants bark. Fans shout. Friends gab. Acquaintances chat. Enemies snarl. Babies wail. Brats whine. Politicians babble. Hoodlums holler.

Lovers whisper.

I think that's why God whispered to Elijah.

The mighty prophet was in a cave. It wasn't the famous cleft in the rock. It was more like a hole in the wall. It was a hiding place. Call it odd—or exasperating—or pitiful. Choose your word. Elijah had just prayed down fire on water-drenched wood. He had laughed last and put his enemies to rest. But when one pagan woman sent a threatening message, the prophet ran for his life. The Lord had sent an angel to help him, but still, in the next scene, the bold man of faith was cowering in a hidden corner of Mount Sinai.

Fear can make even a mighty man look for a cave.

Who hasn't wanted to pull up the covers and stay in bed rather than face a hard day? Who hasn't tried tricks to avoid problems rather than staring down the dilemmas?

Caves come in all shapes and sizes. You can chisel your own personal cave out of any old wound. You can hide in anger, in self-pity, in fear. You can waste a lot of life in your cave. In fact, you can stay in your cave until it becomes your tomb.

God never wants His saints hiding in caves. He sure didn't want Elijah frittering away his life in a hole. Here's what happened: "Then a great and powerful wind tore the mountains apart and shattered the rocks before the LORD." It must have been a twister. But the Bible makes it clear that "the LORD was not in the wind." And Elijah stayed in his cave.

"After the wind there was an earthquake." Giant tectonic plates jerked. Though the cave walls shook, "the LORD was not in the earthquake" and Elijah didn't come out. "After the earthquake came a fire." It was no toe-warming, weenie-roasting campfire. It must have been a wild brush fire ravishing the arid desert floor. But "the LORD was not in the fire" and the prophet was not yet out of his hole.

"And after the fire came a gentle whisper. When Elijah heard it, he pulled his cloak over his face and went out and stood at the mouth of the cave" (1 Kings 19:11–13).

Elijah had failed. The prophet was lost in doubt, wallowing in self-pity. Although he deserved a shout of scorn, he received the whisper of love.

The beautiful, soft voice of God can comfort the most cowering saint.

Husband, if your wife is crying on the pillow next to yours, will yelling at her make her wounds disappear? Mom, if your newborn is screaming in your arms, will shouting back soothe the troubled infant? People in pain need whispers, not shouts. The whisper is the voice of comfort.

*T*he oldest orchestra in the world, the Leipzig Gewandhaus Orchestra, had begun Beethoven's Third Symphony. However, the beauty of the symphony was defiled as a curious dog wandered into the building. The plain, dark dog wandered among the strings, woodwinds, and brass. The mutt blithely ignored the desperate gestures from the stagehands and strolled next to the conductor. Maybe the dog thought the conductor's moving baton was a stick for playing fetch. Maybe he sniffed the leader's leg or slobbered on his polished shoes. I don't know. But the music stopped. The beauty ceased. The sublime symphony gave way to the auditorium's cacophonous laughter.

You might imagine the conductor's wrath. Would he strike the dog with his baton? Or just kick him and shout, "Get!"?

Neither. Instead, the sophisticated director stooped down and scratched the pooch on the scruff of the neck until the dog's tail wagged. He didn't yell at the dog who ruined the symphony— he whispered. I don't know what the maestro said. But the gentle words worked well enough. The dog let the conductor lead him off the stage so the symphony could recommence.[1]

Have you ever felt like a mutt in the midst of God's great symphony? I have. I've interrupted His perfect and beautiful will. I've let his sublime song in me sometimes become a pathetic, panting whimper. I've slobbered sin in the very presence of His holiness. I've hidden in some dark caves. Yet, He hasn't slain me. He hasn't kicked me. He hasn't yelled at me. Instead, the Lord of hosts has knelt time after time to whisper in my ear: *Alan, what are you doing here? I love you. But this isn't where you belong. Come along now—follow Me.* And so I go.

God whispers to His wounded bride. "Comfort, comfort my people, says your God. Speak tenderly to Jerusalem, and proclaim to her that her hard service has been completed, that her sin has been paid for" (Isaiah 40:1–2). When Israel was at her worst, God's plan was to speak softly to her. "'Therefore I am now going to allure her; I will lead her into the desert and speak tenderly to her.... In that day,' declares the LORD, 'you will call me "my husband"; you will no longer call me "my master"'" (Hosea 2:14, 16).

If you're hurting, you may be hearing plenty of condemning shouts. The driver in the next lane might yell at you. Your boss might yell at you. Your own family members might yell at you. But God never hollers curses upon His beloved. He'll correct you, convict you, but never condemn you. God doesn't yell at His bride. God moves His beloved from caves of doubt, fear, and self-pity not with shouts of doom but with whispers of grace.

Amazing isn't it? The blowing, shaking, and burning didn't fish the prophet out of his hole. The still, small voice did.

Every good communicator knows that while a *SHOUT!* pushes a listener away, a whisper draws a listener forward. Whispers make people stop their shuffling in order to lean frontward and cup their ears to hear.

If you are in a dark, emotional cave, God probably is not going to yank you out—He's going to whisper you out. With all the power in the world, He can certainly twist you, shake you, or burn you. But when God wants you near, He'll whisper as lovers do.

After all, if you are really close to someone, there's no need to shout. When I'm a hundred yards away from my wife in a crowd, she'll wave her arms and shout at the top of her lungs, "A-L-A-N!"

When I'm upstairs in our house, Anne doesn't need to shout as loudly, but she still may need to holler, "ALAN—DINNER TIME!" or, more likely, "ALAN, TRASH NEEDS TO GO OUT!" When our little family gathers at the dinner table, we need only enough volume to drown out clanking forks. And when Anne and I are alone at a linen-covered dinner table, our voices grow as soft as the candle's flicker. But at night, after prayer, when she snuggles close, our low voices flicker even softer...and we whisper.

The closer you are, the softer you speak. A bridegroom doesn't shout intimate words from his pillow to the bride in his arms. He whispers them in her ear.

God came close to Elijah. So His voice grew sweet and soft. When God draws near to you, keep a holy hush and wait for His whisper.

To say God whispers doesn't mean He is always quiet. Expect God's whisper, but don't expect a subdued God. Tornadoes, earthquakes, and wildfires can be noisy events. The King of kings intends to announce His glory. "The LORD reigns.... Fire goes before him.... His lightning lights up the world.... The mountains melt like wax before the LORD" (Psalm 97:1, 3–5).

The Holy One of Israel made sure to manifest His awesome majesty to Elijah. But the Lord's instructions were not in the earth, wind, and fire. The collection of awesome, noisy, cataclysmic events was like a shout, but God wasn't in the shout. The manifestations announced His coming, but His message came in the still, small voice that followed.

I like seeing manifestations of God. Someone recently told me he had seen a big angel standing outside his door. Wow! I'd like to see a big angel. In fact, I'd settle for a little angel. I like being astonished by heaven breaking forth on earth. I like seeing people touched by God. I don't need emotionalism, but I relish the earthly evidence of God's supernatural presence. Manifestations are exciting.

But we don't live by the manifestations—we live by the message.

When God sends revival, dramatic signs often accompany it. When John Wesley preached, sometimes people were struck dumb as if in a trance. When Jonathan Edwards preached, sometimes people trembled. When overcome with God's power, sometimes people laugh, sometimes people weep. It's exciting to see God move. But here is history's solemn warning: The surest way to kill a genuine revival is to become so enamored with the Holy Spirit's manifestation that we lose our ears for His message. If we hear His *wh-o-o-sh* but miss His whisper, we'll miss His valuable secrets.

If God does something dramatic in your life, praise Him! But get ready. Grow still. Cup your ears. Lean toward Him. Wait in silent awe. He's sure to whisper something of sweet substance in your ears.

What lovers whisper from their pillows is secret. The heavenly Bridegroom has treasures so intimate and personal to share that He wants to whisper them as if you were the only one listening.

Elijah came to the mouth of the cave. Still lonely, still confused, the prophet stood in the presence of the Lord and listened to the whisper. "But God," the prophet whimpered in essence, "I'm the only faithful one left. I'm all alone."

I doubt God changed His volume or inflection. The Lord kept whispering. *Psst, Elijah, listen closely. I've a secret plan to tell you. Come closer. You're not alone! You will anoint Hazael, Jehu, and Elisha. You'll be amazed at what they will do. And, psst, Elijah, give Me your ear. Listen to this secret: "I reserve seven thousand in Israel— all whose knees have not bowed down to Baal"* (1 Kings 19:14–18).

Imagine a homemaker-wife whose day is coming unglued. The kids are running wild. The youngest has a gloppy nose and a cough that sounds like the croup. The furnace repairman just came by to say that the system can't be fixed; it'll have to be replaced. The dishes are still in the sink, and the dog is tracking mud all over the carpet. To make matters worse, the last thing her husband said on the way out the door was, "I'll be home late tonight. Don't hold dinner for me."

It's not much of a day. Until surprisingly, midafternoon, her husband calls. His voice is quiet. He whispers so the others in his office won't overhear. "Hey, hon. I love you. I miss you. I canceled my late appointment today. I've decided to slip out of here early. I've already lined up a baby-sitter. I'm going to take you out to our favorite restaurant tonight. See you in a few hours."

She hangs up the phone. The house is still full of clamor, but suddenly her heart is full of song. She smiles and starts humming. She knows a secret. Croupy kids and furnaces and dishes and dog tracks are no longer all there is. Her husband has not left her alone—he's thinking of her. He took the time to seek her out, to whisper in her ear. He loves her. He's coming home soon. He has wonderful things planned for her. So she smiles and sings her way through the day.

Some Christians seem to smile and sing their way through life. Yet, if you look at their lives, their circumstances still look crummy. How could it be? Perhaps they've listened to the heavenly Husband's secret whisper: *"Psst,* darling, I love you. This is not all there is. Something better's coming. I'm thinking of you always. I'll be home to get you real soon."

*I*f you're longing to hear God's voice, do not try to figure it out like a spy deciphering a code. Do not sit in the grandstands waiting for God's announcements over the public address system. Instead, remember that you are His bride. Let the last lamp of worldly activity be turned out. Let the clamor of the world's pressures grow silent. Fluff your pillow. Look for the Lord's smile. And listen. *Shh*—He's whispering. Sweet somethings, for your ears only.

WANDERING

CHAPTER FOURTEEN

WITHDRAWING

He went away sad, because he had great wealth.
Mark 10:22

An unnamed man ran full speed to see the Nazarene teacher. Throwing himself at the Rabbi's feet, the desperate man begged for an answer to life's greatest question: "What must I do to live forever?" (Mark 10:17, my paraphrase).

I say he begged because everyone is desperate when asking that question. It's not a casual question. It's not a take-it-or-leave-it question. It is *the* question.

Some call the psychic hotline. Some clip the horoscope from the paper. Some study health books. Some take nineteen vitamins a day. Some jog, walk, or nap. But everyone, in one way or another, is begging for an answer: "What must I do to make my life last?"

The desperate man at Jesus' feet was no slouch. He was rich. He had been a fine Hebrew student who not only knew the law but, since his bar mitzvah, hadn't goofed up once. I'm sure his parents were proud of him. His friends looked up to him. His business associates respected him.

Jesus' answer to the successful young man was, by any standard, dismaying. "One thing you lack," He replied. "Go, sell everything you have and give to the poor" (Mark 10:21).

It was a dismaying answer because Jesus said "everything." Had He said "some things" or "a few valuable things," it would have been challenging enough. But sell everything?

It's dismaying because the kids need the college fund, and someone's gotta pay Grandma's medical bills. It's dismaying because everyone wants to have *something.* It's dismaying because I don't know anyone who has actually sold everything he owns and given the proceeds to the homeless shelter.

So the young man went away sad.

I don't know where he went or if he came back. I don't know if, in his dejection, he joined a pagan cult that accepted much smaller capital contributions or if, in the darkened crucifixion sky, the light shone into his soul.

I like to think I'll ask him about it one day in heaven. I don't know. But this I do know: The day he held on to his riches and walked away from Jesus was not his saddest day. I'm quite sure there was another event in his life that made him even sadder.

I'll explain in a moment. But first, a story about another man who decided to hold back rather than let loose.

'*T*was the season to be jolly, and I had a winning ticket. I should have been full of fa-la-las but I felt more awash in boohoohoos. You'll probably laugh in my face when I tell you this tale. But if you had been pushing my shopping cart that day, you'd have cried too.

Like most men I know, I would choose almost any activity over browsing stores in the shopping mall. It's strange. I get more tired walking in the mall for a few minutes than I do running wind sprints in 90 percent North Carolina humidity on an August afternoon. When my wife asks me to go to the mall, I beg for other, more satisfying options: "Honey, I don't feel quite up to the mall, but perhaps I could clean out the gutters or work on the tax returns?"

But it was Christmas season. I was a seminary student, and final exams were over. I had no excuse not to go. Plus we were going to the fancy mall that had at least one store I really did enjoy: Brookstone. Perhaps you've seen their catalog.

Their inventory is pure gadgetry. They carry such essentials as sonic foot soothers and automatic golf ball tee setters. As much as I hate the mall, I love Brookstone. So after about five minutes of meandering through ladies' apparel, I announced that I knew a great place to find stocking stuffers. I led Anne to Brookstone.

As we walked into the store, an employee handed me a little card. It was a coupon of sorts. It was one of those scratch-to-reveal-the-prize cards. The clerk quickly explained that upon checking out I should present my card. The cashier would scratch away the gray circle to reveal a percentage. I might get 5, 10, even 20 percent off whatever I had purchased. I thought little of the sales gimmick and crammed the card into my pocket.

While I played miniature billiards and peered through the high-powered telescopes, Anne looked over a hodgepodge of potential stocking stuffers. Soon she roused me from the neck-massaging chair to show me something she really wanted.

It was a silver-handled hairbrush. And she loved it.

"Okay," I said. "Time for you to go. Let me do some shopping in here. I'll meet you at Hecht's in thirty minutes."

Anne left me alone to select some Christmas presents for her. I looked again at the three-thousand-dollar telescopes. *How cool it would be to look at the stars,* I mused. *I could see parts of God's handiwork I've never seen.* I drooled over a couple other high-tag items and then went to examine the silver-handled hairbrush.

It seemed ordinary enough to me. Then I saw the price tag. "Thirty-five dollars?" I muttered aloud. "No way! What hairbrush is worth thirty-five dollars?" The only thing unique about it was the silver (chrome, actually) handle. Big deal. *A brush is a brush,* I reasoned. *I'll save those bucks for something she really needs.*

Satisfied with my frugal decision, I headed to the checkout line with two or three low-budget stocking stuffers. The cashier asked for my scratch-to-reveal-the-prize card.

"Oh yeah," I remembered. "I've got it here somewhere." As I dug the card out of my pocket, the cashier reminded me that once she scratched the gray circle, I could not purchase any other items at that discount.

"Sure, I understand," I said with a smile. I saw right through her little sales trick.

She scratched my gray circle. Then, her eyes wide, she stared at my card. "Excuse me, sir," she said with a stutter. "I need to confer with my manager about this."

A few moments later the store manager appeared. The clerk and the manager whispered secrets to one another. I overheard the boss say, "I was told one of these was floating around somewhere." She shrugged her shoulders and whispered, "Just honor it."

Finally the cashier showed me my scratched percentage-off-purchase card. It read: "100%."

"One hundred percent! What does that mean?" I exclaimed.

"It means what it says, sir. Your discount on these items is 100 percent. There will be no charge for the items you've selected."

"Wow! I'm a winner! You mean it's free—totally free?"

"Yes sir. Free. No charge. Not even tax."

I looked at my stocking stuffers and smiled. Then, out of the corner of my eye, I saw the gleam of the silver-handled hairbrush on the shelf.

That's when my fa-la-las turned into boohoohoos.

I could have gotten that brush for free. In fact, I could have scarfed up a couple of free telescopes and a neck-massaging chair to sit in while looking at the stars. All at no charge.

Instead, I walked out with my bargain bag of stocking stuffers. As I looked again at my cheap gifts, I sighed...and also looked at my cheapskate heart.

That's how I know the rich young man who walked away sadly from Jesus was, some time later, even sadder. He, too, would make a wonderful, sad discovery. It might not have come until he appeared before the throne of heaven and saw his life. I hope it happened much earlier. But at some point the successful, moral seeker discovered that Jesus had wanted to give him spiritual riches beyond measure. And at the same time the young man discovered it all would have been free. One day, when the Holy Spirit scratched away the gray cover of the rich man's understanding, he saw a spiritual coupon declaring: "100%."

He would discover that there really were no strings attached. Not even a heavenly tax. He would see grace for what it is—a totally, utterly, unbelievably, 100 percent free gift. And as he looked at his hands full of earthly possessions, he would see the greater gleam of the kingdom's riches. Suddenly he would see his belongings for what they were: a bargain bag of cheap life stuffers. At the same time he would see the joy, freedom, and peace he could have had…for free.

That was the man's saddest moment.

He had made the first mistake of all who drift away from God. He had decided to withhold something that the Bridegroom really wanted. He had decided he had more to gain by holding back than by letting loose. And so instead of risking it all and stepping toward Jesus, he played it safe—and stepped away. Instead of welcoming the heavenly Groom's intimate embrace, he settled for a cordial handshake.

No marriage grows rich when one partner holds back. Intimacy is built upon risky investment. And though kingdom life is 100 percent free, it is only appropriated when clenched fists let go of their tightly held bargain bags.

Holding back is easy to defend. Putting the silver-handled hairbrush back on the shelf was easy to rationalize. It was a subtle offense. I had not spoken a harsh word to my wife. I had not openly rebelled. I had just been stingy. I had decided that I knew best what my wife really needed, and so I withheld the one thing she had openly requested. And as I peered into my freebie bag, I saw the poverty of my soul.

The first mistake we make in relationships is getting cheap. Holding back affection. Refusing to risk it all for real intimacy. Thinking we're better off withholding a little piece of ourselves for the safekeeping.

But hearts are like money. They get only bigger when invested. They are like seed. They sprout only when generously sown.

It's too bad I couldn't have scratched off the gray circle before I took my items to the cash register. And it's sad that the prosperous young law keeper wasn't around to hear Jesus tell His disciples, "No one who has left home or brothers or sisters or mother or father or children or fields for me and the gospel will fail to receive a hundred times as much in this present age...and in the age to come, eternal life" (Mark 10:29–30).

It's sad that the rich man didn't know why Jesus asked him to sacrifice all. Do you know why Jesus asks so much of you? It's not to see you squirm and remind you who's boss. It's not because He needs your time or talents. It's not just to prove your faith and test your commitment.

The answer is simpler than that, and perhaps surprising. Mark reveals why Jesus asked so much of the rich man: "Jesus looked at him and loved him" (Mark 10:21).

Whenever Jesus asks you to give more of yourself, there's one reason: He loves you. That means He not only wants you in heaven one day. He wants more of heaven in you today. You won't know the depth of the heavenly Groom's affection until He has your whole heart. Holding back part of your soul for safekeeping is the first step to spiritual adultery—a step you dare not take.

God loves your whole self. Have you gladly given the Lord whatever He's desired of you? Or is your silver-handled brush still on the shelf?

CHAPTER FIFTEEN

WHEN TRIPPING KEEPS YOU FROM FALLING

Do not despise the LORD's discipline.
Proverbs 3:11

My mom and stepdad, Jack, went on a diet. They were pretty disciplined until one of my mother-in-law's famous cheese braids arrived. The sweet, succulent pastry is almost irresistible. One night Jack found Mom secretly wolfing down the cheese braid.

"What are you doing!" he cried.

Quick-thinking Mom swallowed the last morsel and replied, "I'm just saving you from yourself."

Noble, huh? She knew the temptation would be too great for her dieting husband. Somebody had to eat the cheese bread. Good ol' Mom was willing to make the sacrifice. Since then, I've used the line often to explain a lot of my own noble marital practices. I use it to explain why I have to eat the last piece of pizza on the table. (I'm saving others from gluttony.) I use it to explain why I sometimes have to tell the punch line to the story my wife has begun. (I'm saving her from the story going too long and people losing interest.) I use it to explain why I should choose which movie or TV show to watch. (I'm saving her from choosing a two-thumbs-down dud.)

I'm joking, of course. Well, sort of. After all, it's true. We do need someone to save us from ourselves.

A seventy-year-old, married man hired a private investigator to look for a former girlfriend. I guess he became obsessed with the memory of the girl whom he'd met at a USO dance years earlier when he was in the navy. They'd had a one-week affair that ended abruptly when he shipped out. After the war, he married somebody else and raised a family.

The PI found the old flame in Palm Springs. So the old navy man called her and reacquainted himself. It made him feel like a kid again. She suggested they plan a rendezvous and spend a weekend together, and he readily agreed.

One thing was clear in his mind. He couldn't spend a romantic weekend with his former girlfriend, slopping around in his old bathrobe and worn-out slippers. He had developed a habit of sleeping unclothed, so he had nothing to wear to bed on his adulterous fling. He went down to the department store and purchased new pajamas, a new silk bathrobe, and new slippers.

When he brought the new nightwear home, he thought his wife was at her sister's house. But she wasn't. While he was pulling his new pajamas out of the bag, his wife walked in and exclaimed how pleased she was to see the new stuff. She admitted that she had been really frustrated with the way he'd dressed for all those years.

Now the man's deception grew worse. He had to lie about why he had bought the new pajamas. And, of course, he had to wear them at home that night. He felt awful. Little did he know that he was about to feel even worse. Listen to him describe what happened next.

I have never worn pajamas and am not used to them. That night when I was trying to put them on, I got one leg in and the other leg stuck in the waistband. I hopped around until I lost my balance, and fell backwards in the bathroom and hit my head, knocking myself cuckoo. I cut my head and got a concussion.

The next thing I knew I woke up in the hospital and I couldn't remember why.

My wife brought me several new nightshirts to replace my pajamas, but I couldn't remember why I had pajamas in the first place. Slowly it all came back to me. I called my old girlfriend to explain, but she didn't believe me. She said it was the last time I was ever going to stand her up and slammed down the phone. It's just as well. I'm getting used to sleeping in nightshirts. Old love and new pajamas are dangerous.[1]

The man might not have known it, but he was saved from himself. A good knock on the head was the greatest gift God could have given him at the time. Sometimes life's hard knocks are the very things that save us. Who is this God of ours who trips men in their own pajamas just to save them from adultery?

This is our God who saw Jonah running in the wrong direction and "sent a great wind on the sea, and such a violent storm arose that the ship threatened to break up" just so the sailors would throw him into the water…just so God could save him with a whale…just so Jonah would follow the Lord…just so all of Nineveh would be saved (Jonah 1:4).

This is our God who let Joseph's brothers throw the dreamer into a pit just so he could get sold into slavery…just so the boy would be sent to Egypt…just so God could save the land from famine…just so Joseph could feed his own family…just so the people of Israel would live on...just so Joseph could teach his brothers, "You intended to harm me, but God intended it for good to accomplish what is now being done, the saving of many lives" (Genesis 50:20).

This is our God who blinded Saul on the way to Damascus just so the mighty persecutor of the Christians would have to be led by the hand for three days...just so he would never forget the lesson of humility...just so he could learn that God's grace is sufficient...just so he could be filled with the Spirit...just so he could tell the high and mighty, "when I am weak, then I am strong" (2 Corinthians 12:10)...and just so he could tell the proud, "God chose the foolish things of the world to shame the wise" (1 Corinthians 1:27).

This is our God who heard His Son ask, "May this cup be taken from me?" and answered "No, Son" just so Jesus would go to the cross...just so He would suffer and die...just so He would defeat death...just so you and I would live.

God is a good God. He is a noble Husband. There is no evil in Him. He wants nothing but good for His bride. But He knows you and I are prone to wander. Aren't you glad He's willing to trip you just to save you from yourself? Aren't you amazed that He'd rather wrestle you to the ground than let you self-destruct?

I find it fascinating that God would wrestle Jacob. Perhaps it was an angel doing the wrestling, but Jacob himself said, "I saw God face to face, and yet my life was spared" (Genesis 32:30). For all his life Jacob had struggled and, somehow, always come out on top. He came out of the womb holding on to his twin brother's ankle. He stole Esau's birthright and his father's blessing. He outwitted his father-in-law and became a prosperous livestock farmer.

One night by the Jabbok, Jacob was preparing to reenter the Promised Land. I suppose God wrestled with Jacob just so the patriarch would never forget the source of his blessings. The Lord wrestled the man who had always come out on top just so he'd never forget that the Lord always gives the victory. But mostly, I think God wrestled Jacob for the same reason He wrestled with the Hebrew people and He continues to wrestle with you and me. God would rather stoop to wrestle us than let us wander away from Him in pride. He wrestles us because He wants to keep us. He wrestles us because He wants to be close to us.

I wrestle my little boy a lot. Wrestling is not really my first choice, however. I would rather have Bennett voluntarily wrap his arms and legs around me. I'd like him spontaneously to squeeze me with all his might and tell me how much he loves me. But, unfortunately, three-year-old boys have more exciting things to do than sit around all day hugging their daddies. So if I need a hug and he won't give it to me voluntarily, I'll wrestle it out of him. Sometimes he squeals and squirms. That's all right. I just want the physical contact. I just want to be close to him. He might try to get away, but I'm bigger and stronger than he is. One way or another, I'll get the closeness that I want from him.

If you feel as if you're wrestling with God, has it occurred to you that maybe He's just looking for a little more contact with you?

Hear me plainly, I'm not suggesting that God sends evil. Cancer is no gift. Failure is never fun. But getting wrestled away from sin is a part of God's grace.

A teenage boy in our church was caught with drugs recently. He's a really good kid who made a stupid mistake. He's not a drug addict or a drug dealer. In fact, I'm pretty sure it was his first time toying with marijuana. Sadly, a lot of kids do it regularly. But most don't get caught. As his mother wept telling me the story, she added, "He seems to get caught every time he does something wrong."

You know what we concluded? Wow—God must love that boy a lot. Getting caught is a gift. "My son, do not despise the LORD's discipline and do not resent his rebuke, because the LORD disciplines those he loves, as a father the son he delights in" (Proverbs 3:11–12). May I paraphrase it loosely? "Don't resent little tumbles that keep you from gigantic falls. Don't despise a mild concussion if it keeps you from adultery." Isn't that what Jesus was implying when He said, "If your hand causes you to sin, cut it off"?

*H*ave you bought any new pajamas lately? Have you acquired something new in your life that is designed to lead you away from God? It might be a destructive habit or a fresh lust. It might be an opportunity to get ahead with a shady business deal. It might be a small compromise for the sake of big popularity. I don't know what your new pajamas might look like. They usually look sleek and feel smooth at first, but if they're part of a plan to wander from God, I hope you trip on them.

I once heard an interviewer ask Billy Graham, "How have you kept yourself from temptation? So many nationally known evangelists have fallen into sin, but you have remained above reproach. What has been your secret?"

Graham shocked his interviewer and me with his answer: "Years ago I prayed a simple prayer for God to protect me from bringing scandal to the body of Christ. I told the Lord that if He saw me preparing to bring dishonor to His name that I would like for Him to strike me down. I asked God please to kill me before letting me hurt His name."

Wow! Maybe you can't pray that prayer. I'm not sure I can. But here's one I think we can pray:

"Lord, let me follow You so closely that You never need to send a storm to blow me back to You.

"Lord, let me embrace You so fully that You never need to wrestle me just for intimate contact.

"Lord, let me walk so humbly that You'll never need to squelch my pride with Your blinding light.

"Lord, let me love You so thoroughly that You'll never need to trip me in my own pajamas.

"Lord, no matter what, please save me from myself."

CHAPTER SIXTEEN

LOVE DEFILED

Anyone who chooses to be a friend of the world becomes an enemy of God.
James 4:4

I wish it were not, but the following story is true. I've changed a few details. I'll explain my alterations after I tell you the story.

Isabel had just turned twenty-three when her landlord put her on the street. She had no money, no home, no friends. She had no college education and no income. As she sat on the city bench scouring the want ads, Isabel was looking for more than a job. She was searching for some hope.

That's when Josh noticed her.

"Looking for a job?" he asked pleasantly.

"No, I'm checking my mutual fund's performance," Isabel responded sarcastically. As she looked up from the paper, she was bowled over by her inquirer. He was stunning! His dark suit was custom tailored, his bright shirt was lightly starched, his tie had a tasteful but daring splash of color. Upon seeing the handsome prince, Isabel wished she could retract her sarcasm. "Sure, I am looking for a job. You got one for me?" Then she considered her own appearance. It had been four days since she had really bathed—two days since she had even combed her hair.

"Maybe you could help out in my office," said the handsome man.

No one, not even Josh, knows why he offered Isabel such hope that afternoon. To this day, Josh only says, "I felt strangely attracted to her as she sat lonely and empty on that city bench. Despite her old clothes and disheveled appearance, she looked unusually beautiful to me. I guess I loved her from that very moment."

And how Josh did love her. He not only gave her a job, he taught her the secrets of his business so she could earn a good living on her own. He found her an elegant apartment and paid the deposit and the first month's rent. He lavished her with clothes, jewelry, and perfume. Isabel's once hidden beauty blossomed like a rose atop thorns.

On their first date, Isabel invited Josh in and just about threw herself on the man. She was so grateful to her prince she would have given him anything that night, including her body. But Josh turned down her invitation to the bedroom. He didn't want to be "paid back" for his generosity. He wanted more. He wanted a real relationship. He wanted to know this woman, and he wanted her to know him.

So Josh allowed time to go by so they could talk and their love could develop. Over many months Josh courted her, wooed her, and finally two years later took her hand in marriage.

On their honeymoon Isabel kept saying, "Pinch me! Is this really happening?" Hardly two years before, Isabel had been sitting on a city bench with nothing. Now she had everything. The clothes, the jewelry, the resort honeymoon, the princely husband—all of it was great. But what she really couldn't believe was how happy she felt. Love, joy, hope—she'd never had those things before. Her only fear was that it would be taken away someday. What if, she feared, Josh stopped loving her?

Josh didn't stop loving her. If anything, he loved her more and more as the years went by.

But Bell, as Josh liked to call her, wasn't around as much anymore. She had developed her business skills and started her own little company. Her business often required her to work late or travel out of town. But she was successful, and Josh was proud of her. Isabel not only had become beautiful, she also had become prosperous.

Before she met Josh, hardly anyone knew she existed. Now everyone noticed Isabel, including other men in her office. Especially Jim. He complimented her appearance and told her how much he admired her business savvy. Jim made it a point to smile at Isabel every day.

It seemed harmless for Jim to notice Isabel. But it wasn't harmless when Isabel began to notice Jim. One day she took note of how warm and contagious his smile was. Once, when he wasn't looking, Isabel took a long glance at Jim's physique and wondered how he stayed so fit. One day Isabel and Jim were in the elevator together, and she found herself really enjoying the fragrance of Jim's cologne.

The more Isabel noticed Jim, the more attractive he became to her. He was smart, winsome, funny, successful, and popular. Sometimes at home Isabel would think of something funny Jim had said that day, and she'd chuckle out loud.

Isabel not only liked Jim, but she also enjoyed being liked by him. It was flattering. It made her feel warm all over. It was the same sort of thrill she'd felt when Josh first noticed her on the city bench. Though she wouldn't have admitted it, Isabel really cared what Jim thought of her. She decided to lose a few pounds.

Just want to get in shape, she told herself. But inwardly she kept thinking about the upcoming business conference in Florida where she would lounge by the pool when not in meetings. She knew Jim would be there.

One day at work she looked in the ladies-room mirror and, after applying fresh lipstick, thought to herself, *Wonder if Jim likes this color?* On another occasion Isabel wore a loose blouse to work. She dropped some papers in Jim's office. When she bent to pick them up, Isabel looked to see if Jim was looking. He was.

Slowly Isabel took Jim into her confidence. She sought his opinion about business matters regularly, but one day she asked him if he'd have a cup of coffee with her. She needed to talk to someone. She was dealing with some childhood emotional scars. She shared. He listened. One afternoon Isabel complained about a crick in her neck. Jim did what she hoped he would. He stepped behind her as she sat in her desk chair, made a joke about the new contract being a pain in the neck, and gently massaged her stressed muscles.

When Jim and Bell arranged their first weekend away together, she told Josh she was taking a business trip to pursue a new contract. Her car was in the shop, so she asked to take Josh's car to the out-of-the-way mountain cabin for her rendezvous with Jim. Josh cleaned the car for her and, upon her request, filled the tank with gas. When she slept with Jim for the first time, she wore the gown Josh had given her for their second wedding anniversary.

Bell found pleasure in her adulterous affair. It was exciting. It gave her a feeling of adventure. The two men's simultaneous love made her feel special. For months she led a dual life. She was wife to Josh and mistress to Jim. She played her role of wife quite convincingly. She played her role of mistress quite passionately. She had no intention of giving up her husband—and no plans to give up Jim either.

Her divided life lasted six months. Josh, an extremely smart and discerning man, suspected something was amiss. One Friday he caught an early plane home—and caught them.

When through her tears and anguish she quieted enough to talk, Bell exclaimed, "Josh, this is not what it seems. I love you. You are my husband, my provider, my strength. I don't want to lose you. I'm not sure I could live without you. I want to have children with you. I want to grow old with you."

What Bell said next floored the betrayed husband.

"But I just need some pizzazz in my life. I don't love Jim like I love you. But he makes my life more exciting. You do want me to have an exciting life, don't you, Josh? I love you, but I'm in love with Jim too. Can you understand? I want you both. You're such a good man, Josh. Please bear with me, I'm begging you. Just let me see Jim a little longer until I get it out of my system. I can love you both. I can do it. I can."

When she spoke those last words, "I can do it. I can," a strange, authoritative boldness arose in Josh. He stared his adulterous wife in the eye and spoke slowly and directly, punctuating each word. "No, you can't.

"Bell, my beloved Bell," he continued calmly, "I still love you with all my heart. I loved you the moment I saw you. I'm sure, no matter what, I won't stop loving you. But you have chosen to love another man."

Isabel interrupted, "No, Josh, believe me. I didn't plan this. It just happened."

Josh spoke with that strange, authoritative boldness again. "No, Isabel. *You chose.* I have been here. I've gone nowhere. I have had my arms outstretched, but you chose another's embrace. I saw you distancing yourself from me, but I did not force my love upon you. I will not now, either. I will always love you, but I will not tolerate one day, not one moment, of my wife in another man's bed.

"Bell, *you must choose.* Me or him. It's all of me or none of me. If you're his lover, you're against me. Can't you see that? Nothing, no one, can hurt me more than my wife in another man's bed. When you're with him, you are stabbing my heart. That makes you my foe. That makes you my worst enemy. So, Bell, *you must choose. Right now.*"

Then, softly, ever so softly, Josh continued. "Oh Bell, could I think so little of you that I could allow you to be shared? Could I consider you a commodity available for exchange from lover to lover? Don't you see? You are not a plaything; you are my wife. You are my treasure, my sparkling diamond.

"You have stabbed my heart today. But can't you understand? The only reason it hurts me so bad is because I love you so much."

Isabel prepared to say something about how she hadn't planned on hurting Josh. Instead, she sat in silence. Something he had said stunned her. Something stuck inside her head. In her mind's ear she heard Josh's firm, punctuated words: *No, you can't.* What strange authority her husband's words carried. "No, you can't." Words not of condemnation but of stark truth.

He's right, Isabel thought. *I can't be two men's lover. I can sleep with both men, but I can't actually love both men. To be a lover to one is to be an enemy to the other.*

Then another realization stunned her. *Jim is willing to share me with my husband. He has slept with me even though he has known I'm with Josh most of the time. But Josh won't tolerate a minute of my being with Jim. Jim will share me with Josh, but Josh won't share me with Jim. What does that mean?* Josh's words replayed in her mind: *You are not a plaything; you are my wife.... Could I think so little of you.... You are my treasure.... Could I consider you a commodity... for exchange from lover to lover?*

Suddenly, like a sunbeam from behind a cloud, a wonderful thought came to Isabel. It was a delicious, sweet, powerful, wonderful thought. Her heart leaped, and she smiled as she thought it.

It suddenly made sense. Her husband's exclusive claim over her life was actually an affirmation of her value. "No, you can't." Those weren't words of hate. They weren't spoken out of disrespect. Those were the most loving words anyone had ever spoken to her. Everyone else in her life had treated her as if she were dispensable, as if she could be passed around. Her husband's complete demand for her was a demonstration of how complete his love was for her. His intolerance of Jim indicated the depth of his affection for her.

It all made sense. At the same time, the full, ugly awareness of her sin settled upon her. Isabel knew she had committed adultery. She felt unclean. She felt ugly. She wondered how Josh could ever see beauty in her again. She was a temptress, but her husband had called her a treasure. She was a defiler, but he had called her a diamond.

Her husband's demanding words, "No, you can't," became not a threat but an incredible invitation. It suddenly felt like an opportunity to blossom, a chance to shine. Feeling strangely warm and radiant, Isabel lifted her eyes to see her husband's face. The tears in his eyes brought tears to hers as she let forth the cry of her soul. "Oh Josh, what have I done? What have I done? What have I done? Oh Josh, how can you still love me? Is it possible? Can you really take me back? Oh Josh, how can you? What will you do with your heart that I have stabbed?"

"I will let it bleed," Josh said as he opened his arms to embrace his weeping wife. "I will just let it bleed. It's worth the bleeding to have you back."

I made up the story. But, believe me, the story's true. It's not about a woman named Isabel and a man named Josh. I changed the characters' names. Actually, I just shortened them. Isabel is short for Elizabeth—"pledged to God." Josh is short for Joshua—"the Lord saves."

Maybe you've already guessed who this princely husband is. Joshua is the same name as Yeshua—Jesus. He walked the streets of Jerusalem and the hills of Galilee two thousand years ago in search of His bride. The love of His life was not fitting for a Prince as rich as He. Everyone was surprised at the people He loved and how He loved them. He loved those below the poverty line and introduced Himself to disheveled women. He loved a dying thief and a persistent beggar. He never said *why* He loved who He did. Nor did He take time to evaluate people's worth before He loved them.

This Husband rescued His bride from the bench of despair and gave her what she needed most—Himself. He gave her a purpose and the inward gifts to fulfill that purpose. He gave her love and hope. His greatest delight was making her joy full. He always loved her. He never stopped loving her.

You know Josh is Jesus. But Isabel—the pledged one—who is she? It's easy to look in the newspaper and point the finger at some fallen saints. It's not hard to find some hypocrites in the pews. But who is Isabel, really? Is she…me? Could she be…you?

Before you answer too quickly, read the words of James.

You want something but don't get it.… You do not have, because you do not ask God. When you ask, you do not receive, because you ask with wrong motives, that you may spend what you get on your pleasures. You adulterous people, don't you know that friendship with the world is hatred toward God? Anyone who chooses to be a friend of the world becomes an enemy of God. Or do you think Scripture says without reason that the spirit he caused to live in us envies intensely? (James 4:2–5)

If you're like most, you have different sorts of friends. You may enjoy shopping with one friend or playing tennis with another. You may vacation with certain friends and play bridge with others.

But the Lord won't be a part-time pal. He is not an occasional buddy. He is your Husband. His love for you is too great to share you. He will not pass you around from lover to lover. To become a "friend of the world" is, in His eyes, to become an adulteress.

Isabel didn't just jump into bed with Jim. She first became his friend. And, step by step, her friendship with Jim became enmity to Josh.

James spells out the steps to spiritual adultery.

Step 1: "You want something but don't get it."

Spiritual lust begins like Isabel's—a quiet notice of the world's appeal. A glimpse of how brightly gold can glitter. A chuckle at how tasteless jokes can draw a crowd. An observation of how broadly popularity can smile. It doesn't take much to start a friendship with the world. Just a peek at its false pleasures can start the cycle.

Step 2: "You do not ask God."

How did Josh feel when his wife sought the counsel of another man? How does a mother feel when her daughter wants to cry on someone else's shoulder? How does a father feel when his son asks some other kid's dad to teach him how to hit a ball?

Noticing the world's physique is soon followed by the desire for the world to notice yours. It doesn't mean you have a mad lust for fame and popularity. It might mean you just want to please people more than you want to please the Lord. It means you inwardly value the opinion of your neighbors more than the opinion of your God. When you stand in front of the mirror, what do you wonder: *How will I look to others today?* Or, *How will I look to God today?*

The more Isabel cared about Jim's approval, the less she cared about her husband's desires. The more she confided in Jim, the less she confided in Josh.

Whose counsel are you seeking to solve your dilemmas? Where are you seeking the answers to your life questions? Your bank account? Your reputation? Your personal contacts? Or your Lord?

Step 3: "When you ask, you do not receive, because you ask with wrong motives, that you may spend what you get on your pleasures."

Some prayers are not prayers at all. They are announcements to God about our intentions with the hope He will endorse our plans. "Let me borrow Your car, Lord, on the way to my prearranged rendezvous." Petitions to help us carry out our will are not prayers at all.

he pleasures of the world are delightful for a season. "Just a little pizzazz for the long, straight race of life," the friend of the world rationalizes. "Surely," the spiritual adulteress pleads, "I can keep running this race and add a little of the world's delights along the way. Surely, Lord, You want me to have an exciting life."

"I love You, Lord," the spiritual adulteress sings on Sunday morning. "I want You. You are my God, my strength, my hope. I have no intention of giving You up. I want to be Yours forever. You are my eternal security. I don't love the world the way I love You. I just enjoy its occasional embrace. Surely You understand, Lord. Can't I have you both?"

With eternal authority God punctuates each word: *No, you can't. I have loved you with an everlasting love, but you have chosen another lover.*

"But, God, I didn't choose. I just drifted this way. It just happened."

You didn't drift—you chose. Read My Word again: "Anyone who chooses to be a friend of the world…." My arms are still extended to you. I have loved you always. I never will stop loving you. But I will not tolerate for one minute My beloved in the arms of another. You cannot belong to Me and belong to the world. My heart is rent asunder by your unfaithfulness. "Do you think Scripture says without reason that the spirit he caused to live in us envies intensely?"

That's how strongly God puts it to you and me: *I will not tolerate for even one moment My bride in the bed of the world. I love you. I always have, I always will. Could I think so little of you as to share you? Could I consider you a commodity to be passed around from lover to lover? How could I, the Lord God, your Maker, your Husband, share you with the devil? I cannot. I will not.*

*I*t's a complete, total demand. But please consider it as Isabel did. It is not a condemnation; it is an invitation. Doesn't it make sense? God's exclusive claim over your life is an incredible affirmation of your value.

"No, you can't." Always remember: Those are the most loving words anyone has ever spoken to you. The Tempter treats you as if you are dispensable—as if you can be passed around. But God's complete demand for you just shows how complete His love is for you. His intolerance of your sin merely indicates how high His affection is for you.

Though you fall to temptation, He calls you a treasure. You know yourself to be a defiler, but He calls you a diamond.

"No, you can't." Hear those words not as a threat but as an invitation. It is an opportunity to blossom, a chance to shine. Do you not feel strangely warm and radiant to consider it? Lift your eyes toward your heavenly Groom's face. Let His tears be overcome by yours. "Oh Lord, what have I done? What have I done? Oh Lord, how can You still love me? Is it possible? Can

You really take me back? Oh Lord, how can You? What will You do with Your heart that I have stabbed?"

I will let it bleed, God says as He opens His arms to embrace His weeping bride. *I will just let it bleed. It's worth the bleeding to have you back.*

I don't know why He would bleed for you or me. I can't figure out why He forgives. But this we know: His demand is great because His love is great. So if you want God to be your Lover, it's only Him or none of Him. Choose now. Choose wisely. The world may promise you passing pizzazz, but only God will be the eternal Lover of your soul.

CHAPTER SEVENTEEN

GLUING IT BACK TOGETHER

Blot out my transgressions.
Psalm 51:1

The honeymoon was over. The birdseed in my boxer shorts proved I'd indeed gotten married. The red crawfish refrigerator magnet proved I'd been on a honeymoon to New Orleans. My wife's hymn singing and smiling as she worked in the kitchen proved I'd married the right woman. And the gas grill proved the honeymoon was over.

I'm sure my brothers thought themselves generous when they gave me a gas grill for a wedding present. But if they'd really loved me, they'd have given me an *assembled* gas grill. As the youngest of three boys, I had received plenty of torture at the callous hands of my brothers. My oldest brother beat me at every sport to remind me who I was. My middle brother beat me at everything else to keep me in my place. But giving me an unassembled gas grill was probably the cruelest thing they ever did to me.

I (actually, *they*) should have forked out the twenty-five dollars and paid the store to assemble the grill. But I was a youth ministries director at the time, and nobody makes less money than youth directors except gas-grill-assembly-instruction writers. I was an English major in college, so at least I should have been able to read the assembly instructions. Unfortunately the assembly instructions were not written in English. Oh, sure, they used actual English words like "tube 1-a" and "1/4-inch wing nut." But phrases such as "Connect ignition switch bracket to 1/8-inch ground screw" clearly are not the English language.

I knew my literary and religious studies would offer me no help in assembling the grill. Admittedly, I have been mechanically challenged ever since junior high industrial arts. Nonetheless, I spread the 1,002 gas-grill parts across the whole downstairs of our apartment and began assembling.

*I*t was a bad time for me to be assembling. We had been married less than two weeks. We hadn't even settled into the apartment, much less settled into married life, and gas-grill assemblage brings out the ugliest character traits in me: fits of rage, total obsession, and foaming at the mouth. I should have waited for a more opportune time to put the cooker together— perhaps the week after our last child goes to college or the first week of retirement. But no man should assemble a gas grill the first week after his honeymoon.

So I was already seething when Anne returned from her first married trip to the grocery store. She was excited about her purchases—bread, canned goods, ground round, salt and pepper, ice cube trays, toothpicks, that sort of thing. Stocking the kitchen should have been a joyful celebration of our new life together. But, given my grill-assembling mood, I didn't celebrate her purchases—I scrutinized them.

"Sugar! What do we need that for? Deodorant! How much do you sweat?"

Well, I exaggerate a little. I didn't question the sugar or the anti-perspirant. But I flew off the handle when I saw the cutting board.

The cutting board was a twelve-inch-by-sixteen-inch construction of laminated wood with little plastic feet on its underside. Although it wasn't corkboard, it was no oak butcher block, either. As best I remember, it cost about fifteen bucks.

"Honey! A cutting board! Who said we needed that? We can't afford this butcher block. Take it back!"

Anne didn't say much. She just stopped her hymn singing and smiling and quietly stocked the kitchen shelves. I snarled at her one more time and returned to part #203 of the gas grill.

A few hours later while I was on part #204, I heard a curious, high-pitched squeaking noise. The sound was somewhere between an angry mosquito and a wet log hissing over a hot fire. The long, sustained shrill aroused Anne's curiosity as well. She began searching the kitchen for its source. Soon we heard a loud *pop*.

"What was that, honey?" I asked.

"Oh—nothing," she mumbled as she made a quick exit from the kitchen.

My grim-faced grill construction kept me distracted enough that I didn't figure out the source of the odd noise. It was, of course, the cutting board. Anne had not taken it back to the store as I had strongly suggested. Instead, she had washed it thoroughly. Evidently the water had penetrated the laminate, expanded the wood, and split our new cutting board in two.

Feeling herself in mortal danger, Anne did not tell me about the split cutting board until I had undergone the mandatory grill-assembly cooling-off period. A day or two later she confided to me that she had discovered the board to be the source of the mosquito-like squeak, had thrown a towel over it, and when it popped, had sneaked it upstairs to hide it. After it finished splitting wide open, she had pitifully attempted to glue it back together.

Anne learned two truths that day: Elmer's glue can't keep a cutting board together, and hiding problems can't keep a marriage together. Risky self-disclosure is the only path to intimate marriage. So she chose her moment, and she told me.

Upon seeing her penitent heart and hearing her quaking voice, I learned some lessons that day too. I learned

> *...if my wife is gladly willing to do a chore I cringe to do, such as grocery shopping, don't condemn her in the process;*
>
> *...if she finds a little joy in buying some small household item, it's not because she wants to waste our money but because she is making a nest for us. I get to enjoy a nest I didn't make and eat the chicken fillets that were trimmed on the cutting board I didn't want;*
>
> *...a song in a wife's soul and a smile on her face is worth more than a thousand butcher blocks.*

But mostly I learned that when I've been a grouchy, growling, grill-assembling ogre, there's only one way to be restored: saying "I'm sorry."

If you want to learn about the greatest kind of confession, it makes sense to hear it from the lips of the greatest kind of sinner.

The Bible tells us David was "a man after God's own heart." It wasn't because as a shepherd boy he had killed a menacing giant. It wasn't because as a harpist he had soothed the king's migraines. It wasn't because as a general he had won so many battles. And it certainly wasn't because the king of Israel had no sin.

It was the spring of the year, "the time when kings go off to war" (2 Samuel 11:1), when David first saw Bathsheba. Oh, if only the king of Israel had been at battle with his men! He would not have been in a position to lust after another man's wife had he been in the war zone. Why do we sin most readily when the real battle is distant? Betrayal rarely begins on the noble fields of the spiritual battle's front line. It so often starts in stupid places that shouldn't be stressful in the first place. In simple shopping purchases. In grill assembly. David would have been better off with a sword in hand on the battleground than with a martini in hand on the royal couch.

With no spiritual armor on, King David put down the evening newspaper and stepped onto the balcony for a breath of fresh air. From his lofty palace rooftop, the king could look into others' backyards. The king saw things he shouldn't have been able to see. Bathsheba was a bathing beauty, but she was no seductress. She just wanted to get clean. David just wanted to get her, and when he did, his heart became unclean.

David tried to cover up his sin but couldn't. So he arranged for Bathsheba's husband to be killed in battle. Lust. Adultery. Conspiracy to murder. How could this king be a man "after God's own heart"?

David was such a man because the one thing he couldn't stand was distance from the heart of God. There was only one way back to God. He knew how to say "I'm sorry." His confession is recorded in Psalm 51.

> Have mercy on me, O God,
>> according to your unfailing love;
> according to your great compassion
>> blot out my transgressions....
> I know my transgressions,
>> and my sin is always before me....
> Surely I was sinful at birth....
> Cleanse me...
>> wash me....
> Create in me a pure heart, O God...
> The sacrifices of God are a broken spirit...
>> and contrite heart.

"I'm sorry." Period. David offered God no "I'm sorry, but..." No "I'm sorry, but You know the pressures of being king." No "I'm sorry, but You can see how beautiful Bathsheba is." Just "I'm sorry...I know my transgressions...I was sinful at birth...Oh, I'm so sorry, Lord."

Nor did David offer God "I'm sorry. Let me make it up to You." He knew sacrifices do not pay God back. He knew we can't make it up to God. Instead of burnt offerings, the king offered a broken and contrite heart.

And notice, David offered no quick, superficial "I'm sorry, I'm sorry" with the hopes of avoiding pain. He wanted cleanliness, not comfort. The man after God's own heart wanted more than anything else to be close to the heart of God. He didn't seek the removal of sin's consequences nearly so much as the removal of his barrier to seeing God's face.

"I'm sorry." Period.

That's what I had to learn to say the second week of my marriage. I couldn't blame my grouchiness on my grill. I couldn't make up for my growling with a spending spree. I couldn't gloss it over with a quick apology. I had to learn to say, "I'm sorry." Period. And I would have to keep learning to say it. I had to practice saying it the second year of my marriage and the twelfth year. I'm sure I'll rehearse it again my twenty-second year as well as my sixty-second year.

My problem isn't in a grill, it's in me. It's called sin. And there's only one way back when you've growled at the one you love: "I'm sorry."

I'm not sure what aggravations or disappointments have made your heart self-centered. I don't know what earthly dilemmas have caused you confusion. I don't know what might have distanced you from your heavenly Groom. But of this I'm sure: The Lord owes you no apology. There's only one pathway to restoration and intimacy with the One you love. Stop. Step away from the grill. Get your ears off the shrill sound of splitting circumstances, and listen to the tone of your own heart. I'm sure you'll see it. There's only way back to God. Say "I'm sorry, Lord." Nothing more. Nothing less. "I'm sorry."

WALKING

My Champion

My Advocate

New Every Morning

Finding Your First Love

Walking in His Love

Loose-Dirt Longings

A Husband's Good Night

CHAPTER EIGHTEEN

MY CHAPMION

As a bridegroom rejoices over his bride,
so will your God rejoice over you.
Isaiah 62:5

an you imagine a bunch of husbands competing to see who can praise his wife best?

I wanted to see it for my own eyes. I wanted to hear it with my own ears. So I staged a contest. It took place on a Wednesday night after the church fellowship dinner. The instructions were simple: "Write down five reasons why you have the best wife in the world. Read it to your wife in front of the congregation. Listeners will judge your words by their applause. The husband getting the most cheers will win a nice dinner for two at a local restaurant."

I doubted many would dare an attempt. After all, most men have a hard time expressing their feelings, especially in front of several hundred people. Besides, they had almost no time to prepare their compliments. I considered recruiting a few eloquent husbands just to make sure my little contest wasn't a total bomb. But, as it turned out, there was no need to seed the game. I had underestimated the men of my church.

Half joking, I opened the contest with a mocking sense of urgency in my voice: "I'll only take five husbands—the first five—only five. Come now, quickly."

You might not believe it, but men began leaping from their seats all over the fellowship hall. They raced toward the platform like Olympians. Seven of the men refused to leave the stage. I couldn't turn such eager husbands away.

David went first. According to my directions, his wife, Sherri, stood. The microphone shook mildly as he began. "I have the most wonderful wife in the world because…," his voice cracked, "she forgave me and stood by me when…" Tears wet his face. Men grew still and swallowed hard. Women watched and wept.

Some cried because they longed to hear their own mate utter such words. Some cried because they were praying for God to give them such a partner. Some sat silently as people do in the presence of awesome affection.

After the church erupted in applause for David, the next husband spoke while his wife also stood. "Becky, you're the most wonderful wife in the world because…," and *his* voice broke. In all, seven men took the microphone. Five portrayed the picture of blessing with their tears. Two painted it with a brush stroke of beautiful words. The congregation erupted in nearly equal applause each time. What I had designed to be a fun little contest in the middle of my Wednesday teaching became my whole message. And what a message it was.

It was a rare and splendid sight. Men competing to proclaim their love for their wives. Husbands rejoicing over their brides—so publicly, so extravagantly. It rebutted the locker-room macho men who brag about their ability to use women rather than love them. It renounced the businessman making wisecracks about his wife at the office party.

Our little "Praise Your Wife" competition touched the most

tender longing within the human heart. Don't we all crave someone to praise us publicly? What woman doesn't long for such an advocate? Don't you relish someone so faithful, so passionate, that he would sprint to the platform just for a chance at the loudspeaker to announce his approval of you? And, men, how much more do we long for someone to champion our causes? We love to bask in another's undaunted approval.

With a little pastoral pride, I thought if anyone asked me what kind of church I pastored, I now had a fine reply: "The kind of church in which husbands compete to bless their wives." I drank in the evening as I listened to the words of grace, felt the emotion of the men on the platform, and quietly composed my own, personal praise list.

Anne, you are the most wonderful wife in the world because

...after twelve years of marriage, every time we leave a church meeting or a family gathering or a social party, I still smile and think, Wow, I get to go home with you.

...your abiding trust in God was the womb in which my intimacy with Him was born.

...you paint a picture of blessing over my life daily—and it is a masterpiece.

...your heart is wide enough to harbor hundreds of ships from stormy seas, and yet, somehow, you have room for my battered sails at any time.

...you are the master Mom. If you'd not had a chance to mother, it would have been as though Michelangelo had no stone and chisel, as though Rembrandt had no paint and canvas.

It was a wonderful sight—men rejoicing over their women. But the best sight in the house was not the grooms speaking; it was the brides standing. I didn't watch the men at the microphone. I watched their wives instead. I watched the beloved as they allowed the ascriptions of their husbands' affection to fall like dew at dawn. I watched the wives as they drank in their husbands' words of life like nectar. I watched the objects of the husbands' joy because there is no more beautiful sight than a woman receiving her husband's rejoicing.

You may never have been the beneficiary of an earthly "praise your spouse" contest. In fact, you may have heard more words of cursing than blessing over your life. The sin-crushed world is quick to curse. It takes no effort for a family member, or a friend, or a spouse, or a boss to find your flaws. The fallen creation of God finds it second nature to point out the ugly. Few earthlings know how to bless.

If you long for someone to take joy in you, here's good news: "For the LORD will take delight in you, and your land will be married.... As a bridegroom rejoices over his bride, so will your God rejoice over you" (Isaiah 62:4–5).

Read those words over and over until they sink in. Do you see it? Do you believe it? Regardless of your earthly, flaw-finding friends, you really do have a Champion.

How does a bridegroom rejoice over his bride? He believes in her. He is her chief advocate and protector. He sees only the best in her as if he's blind to her flaws. He is proud to have her on his arm. He can't wait to be alone with her. Nothing else matters to him but the joy and well-being of his bride. The bridegroom celebrates. He dances. He sings. He feasts.

ow can Jesus rejoice over you? His nails killed your sin. He took the curse so the blessing would be yours. He saw the depths of hell so He wouldn't have to see it in you.

Early on, Bob and Helen's marriage was pretty bad. In fact, they considered giving up. But instead of calling it quits, they came up with a great idea. Here's how Bob describes it.

"We decided to make a list of all the things we didn't like about each other. Of course, it was hard, but Helen gave me hers, and I gave her mine. It was tough reading.

"Next we did something which might seem foolish, so I hope you won't laugh. We went to the trash basket in the backyard and we burned those lists of bad things. We watched them go up in smoke and put our arms around each other for the first time in a long while.

"Then we went back into the house and made a list of all the good things we could dig up about each other. This took some time since we were down on our marriage. But we kept at it, and when we finished, we did another thing which might look silly."

After composing their little praise list for one another, Bob and Helen framed the hand-scribbled lists and hung them on their bedroom wall.

"We agreed to read these things at least once a day," Bob continued. "Of course, we know them by heart now. When I hear fellows complain about their wives, I think of my list.... When I really understood [Helen's] good points, I tried all the harder to build on these. Now I think she's the most wonderful person in the world.... That's all there is to it!"[1]

Two thousand years ago when the nails went into the

Messiah's wrists, blood flowed, the earth quaked, the sky darkened, the temple curtain tore, and God burned up your whole bad list. At the same time the Lord quickly wrote out a list of everything He loves about you. I guess it's hanging on a mansion wall in heaven. I'm sure He knows the list of virtues by heart.

*J*ust for fun, imagine your church is hosting a "Bless Your Spouse" contest. You take the last bite of Brunswick stew, speak to someone from your Sunday school class, and wait for the program to begin. The pastor announces the contest rules: "Each husband will be allowed only five compliments. The bride must stand and listen to her husband's public praise. The winner gets a fine meal at a local restaurant. The microphone will be given to the first husband who makes it to the platform. On your mark, get set, go!"

To your surprise, men jump up from their seats and begin clambering toward the stage. Amid the commotion, a strange sight emerges. A soft but brilliant light begins to shine on the platform. Is it some clever stage light? No. It is brighter and purer than any earthly light you have ever seen. Several husbands try to jump into the luminous area, but they quickly realize that it's no limelight. Something makes the men aware that they don't belong in that spot. It is holy.

The congregation grows silent. Your heart thumps wildly. No man takes the microphone, but a voice resonates over the loudspeakers. The voice is awesome and yet strangely comfortable to your ears. It is clear that Jesus is speaking. Though you can't see His face, you can hear the smile in His voice as He gladly announces: *I have the most wonderful bride in the world. I'd like her to stand, please.*

You are the bride of Christ. It is your turn to stand. It is time to let His praise and affection fall upon you. It is time for your Savior to tell all the listening world why He believes in you.

I have the most wonderful bride in the world because

...you are a gift to Me; I've had my eye on you since before the world was created. I knew you were Mine, and I could hardly wait to have you (Ephesians 1:4).

...you let Me into your life. You are so much a part of Me that it feels as if you are My own body (1 Corinthians 12).

...you're so beautiful to Me that I can hardly take My eyes off you. When I look at you, I can't find a single stain or blemish—I can't even find a wrinkle (Ephesians 5:25–27).

...I can see that you're more than a conqueror. Why, you'll do even greater things than I have done (Romans 8:37; John 14:12).

...you come from a great family. I know there's royalty in your blood (1 Peter 2:9). *And, by the way, I think your Father's the greatest.*

The applause is so thunderous that you look around you. Angels are standing to cheer. It's obvious that your Husband has won the praise contest. Don't be bashful. Step forward to accept your award. A gift certificate to the marriage feast of the Lamb.

CHAPTER NINETEEN

MY ADVOCATE

*We have one who speaks to the Father
in our defense—Jesus Christ.*
1 John 2:1

o have and to hold...for better or for worse..."
It's a gigantic promise that tells the world

...I'll hold you because you're mine, not because everything's fine.
...My hugs work as well in the pit as they do on the pinnacle.
...If even the whole world walks away, I'll stand by your side.
...I am your chief advocate.

"For better or for worse." That's the vow the heavenly Bridegroom made to His bride: "I am with you always, to the very end of the age" (Matthew 28:20). It was the solace of apostle John's soul when he wrote: "If anybody does sin, we have one who speaks to the Father in our defense—Jesus Christ" (1 John 2:1). It was the pillar of Paul's theology: "If God is for us, who can be against us?...Who will bring any charge against those whom God has chosen? It is God who justifies. Who is he that condemns? Christ Jesus, who died—more than that, who was raised to life—is at the right hand of God and is also interceding for us" (Romans 8:31, 33–34).

Christ always takes the side of His bride. That's why He

promised to send the disciples an Advocate: "I will ask the Father, and he will give you another Counselor to be with you forever—the Spirit of truth" (John 14:16–17). The word is *paracletos*. It was a legal term meaning a "helper in court." A paracletos was someone who defended those who were accused and pled their cases before the judge.

The Holy Spirit is a lot like—dare I utter it?—a great lawyer.

Wait! Don't gulp at the scriptural analogy and think of your latest ambulance-chasing-lawyer joke. The people who tell a lot of lawyer jokes are usually those who've never needed a good attorney. (I try not to tell lawyer jokes because lawyers also know a lot of preacher jokes.)

Besides, my oldest brother is a really good lawyer. Even as a kid, he always had a great sense of fairness. Now, with all his education and legal experience, he's become so clever that he almost always wins. Though our shared blood makes me a little biased, I'm sure if I were ever in legal trouble, I'd want David Wright standing between me and the judge.

The following unbelievable story helps illustrate why.

A Christian woman sought David's counsel. David works in a big, fancy firm mostly for big, corporate clients. So when Mary called him about her little real estate dilemma, I'm sure David was hesitant to become too involved. But pure-minded Mary was in his church, and David's heart went out to her.

The single, thirty-four-year-old saint worked at a local crisis-assistance ministry. Over the years she had saved enough to buy a small house for about fifty thousand dollars. Maybe you've felt the joy of being a first-time home owner. The first week can be great fun—hanging pictures, positioning knickknacks, stocking the kitchen, arranging furniture, opening your first mail.

But Mary's fun was rudely interrupted when she discovered a disturbing letter from the city. The memo explained municipal plans for solving her neighborhood water runoff problem. What water problem? The seller hadn't mentioned anything about the yard flooding. After some inquiry, Mary learned that the city planned to fix the problem by burying bigger pipes in her backyard. But each homeowner in the neighborhood was being asked to cough up about a thousand dollars. That was a lot of money that Mary didn't have.

She checked with the city utility department. Evidently the previous owner had complained vehemently about flooding in his backyard. In fact, the city had a letter on file from the former property owner describing the backyard river.

That's when Mary called my brother for advice.

It was a simple case, David figured. By law, the owners had been obligated to disclose such information but instead had hidden it. Mary wasn't seeking fraud damages. She just wanted some help paying for the new storm pipes. David decided to write a simple letter to the previous owner asking him to pay three hundred dollars toward the thousand-dollar city assessment. He was shocked when the previous owner's attorney wrote back offering to pay only fifty dollars.

Baffled, perturbed, and knowing no alternative, David filed a lawsuit.

A judge held a settlement conference. David asked for three thousand dollars on behalf of his client. The sellers refused any settlement and made no counteroffer.

"If you're so confident that you've done nothing wrong," David argued, "why don't you just give my client her money back and sell the house to someone else? If your house is as valuable as you say, you should have no problem selling it again."

No way. No discussion. No settlement. No cooperation.

The little letter requesting three hundred dollars that my busy attorney brother had written out of the goodness of his heart resulted in a week-long trial. By then, David had many hours invested in the little case. There was no way Mary could afford the attorney fees. David knew he was doing it for free. But he didn't care. His dander was up. He was acting out of compassion to help right a wrong. He had become Mary's advocate.

You'll find the sequence of events that followed hard to believe. But every word is true.

David made sure the jury understood how bad the flooding problem was. He called an expert real estate witness who testified that, because of the water problem, Mary's house was worth twelve thousand dollars less than what she had paid for it. One of Mary's neighbors told the jury that one day after a big rain he looked in the backyard and saw his beagle treading water!

In the midst of the trial, the judge called the counselors to his bench and asked them again to settle. David offered to end it for five thousand dollars.

No way. No discussion. No settlement.

It didn't take the jury long to decide that it was an open-and-shut case. They found that the seller had sold the house fraudulently and awarded Mary twelve thousand dollars.

But the story gets better.

In the midst of the trial, the city announced that a new, citywide tax was imposed to fund municipal water and sewer improvements. Mary's neighborhood was first on the list for new pipes. The defendants tried to get the suit dismissed on the grounds that Mary's water problem was going to be fixed by the city for free. But, because of a law that defines fraud damages only by the date on which the fraud occurred, the judge ruled that information about the city's decision to fix the problem was inadmissible. The jury never heard about the free pipes. As the trial proceeded, the city proceeded to fix Mary's problem for free.

The sellers heard the verdict but said they wouldn't pay the twelve thousand dollars. They were going to appeal.

By then, Mary's advocate was building steam. Unruffled, my brother filed a claim that might allow the court to award attorneys' fees and triple fraud damages if the case was deemed to be a deceptive act of commerce. (Here, David told me some legal stuff I didn't understand—about how the sale of a personal home ordinarily is not considered an act of commerce. But through some legal maneuvering, he thought he might pull it off.) Anyway, David told the defendant's counsel that if they continued with the appeal, he would seek an award three times as high as the original damages.

No discussion. No holding back. It went to the appellate court.

The state court of appeals quickly found that the lower court's decision had been proper. Additionally, by a legal quirk related to the seller being a licensed real estate agent, the house sale was deemed an act of commerce. Not only did the appeals court uphold the previous damages award, they tripled the amount: thirty-six thousand dollars. At the same time the court awarded attorney's fees in the amount of forty-five thousand dollars.

The man sold his home fraudulently for fifty thousand dollars. Instead of admitting wrong, he defended his deception—to the tune of eighty-one thousand dollars. Mary, who wanted only three hundred dollars, received thirty-six thousand dollars—and her pipes were installed for free!

Shortly thereafter, because of some downsizing, Mary lost her job with the local crisis ministry. But because she had over thirty thousand dollars in the bank, she managed just fine until she found another job. David says she really likes her house, and her backyard is really dry.

As David finished the tale, I laughed out loud and said, "Wow, what a great story!" And then I looked at my oldest brother's gentle smile, and as I saw his compassionate heart again, I thought, *Wow. What a great advocate.*

That's when I thought of Jesus, our Advocate, contending for us in the heavenlies. I saw a picture of the Paracletos, the Holy Spirit, who comes alongside us to defend us and shine light on the deceptive, fraudulent idols of this age.

One thing's for sure. If Mary had spoken for herself, she would have gained nothing. Mary couldn't plead her own case. With no advocate in the courtroom, she would have walked away with nothing but a soggy backyard.

An advocate is someone who speaks on behalf of another.

That's what your heavenly Advocate does.

Jesus warned His disciples that they would be persecuted and arrested. The backyard floods of life would surely arise. Trials would come. But Jesus assured them, "When they arrest you, do not worry about what to say or how to say it. At that time you will be given what to say, for it will not be you speaking, but the Spirit of your Father speaking through you" (Matthew 10:19–20).

Jesus is pleading your case before the Judge. The One who died for you now stands in heaven's courtroom. He knows exactly what to say. "Father, bless my bride. I have a complaint against her previous property owner. That deceiver defrauded her of her home in Eden. The father of lies has sold my bride a swamp, and I want her paid back. I know she shouldn't have bought it. But— look, Father! The flood is rising! I plead on her behalf. Bless her, Father. Once is good—why not triple her blessing! Give to her more than she could ever imagine or think possible. Make her cup run over. Make her heart overflow with hope. Give her joy unspeakable. Grant her peace that transcends understanding."

Mary had a great advocate in my brother. But David doesn't compare to our heavenly Advocate. There's a big difference in the way damages are awarded in earthly courts versus the heavenly one. When the jury found the swampy-house seller guilty of fraud, the convicted defendant had to fork out the thirty-six thousand dollars. But when the divine Judge announced the defeat of the devil, our Advocate paid the damages Himself. Mary's advocate was generous, but our Advocate gave the unthinkable—on the cross.

"To have and to hold." Your Husband has you. He's holding

you. "For better or for worse." When the flood rises to its highest, your Advocate comes closest. Whatever your trial, don't give up. You'll not be treading water forever. You have the best Counselor in the world speaking on your behalf. He's taken particular interest in your case. After all, He's your Husband.

I'd better be quiet now. Court's in session. Listen. He's beginning His closing argument: "My prayer is not that you take them out of the world but that you protect them from the evil one. They are not of the world, even as I am not of it. Sanctify them by the truth…" (John 17:15–17).

CHAPTER TWENTY

NEW EVERY MORNING

His compassions never fail. They are new every morning.
Lamentations 3:22–23

*A*n elderly couple sat across the breakfast table on the morning of their fiftieth wedding anniversary. The husband put down the paper and spoke to his wife: "After fifty years of marriage, I've found you tried and true."

Unfortunately the aging wife was hard of hearing. "Eh? What's that you say?"

The man spoke louder. "I said, 'After fifty years of marriage, I've found you tried and true!'"

"What?" the wife complained over her squeaking hearing aid.

Nearly shouting, the husband tried again: "AFTER FIFTY YEARS OF MARRIAGE, I'VE FOUND YOU TRIED AND TRUE!"

The old wife lifted her nose and snooted, "Well, after fifty years of marriage, I'm tired of you, too."

A bride must never tire of her husband.

My wife's uncle, one of the ministers officiating our wedding service, was in town only long enough to give us one piece of premarital counsel. He told us a story that has stayed with us ever since.

"When my wife, Joella, and I were on our honeymoon, we had a memorable meal at a good restaurant. During the course of the evening I observed the other couples in the dining room. Most of them hardly spoke to one another. Some pairs rarely even looked at one another. They just sat there, bored and uninterested in the spouse who sat across the table.

"But one couple was altogether different. Though they were both advanced in years, they hardly took their eyes off one another throughout their meal. They leaned forward, gazing across the dinner table. Unmindful of others, they whispered some, smiled some, giggled some, and occasionally just laughed out loud.

"When Joella and I had finished our dinner, I wanted to meet the infatuated couple," Stanley continued. "I figured they were newlyweds. I wanted to hear their story. Perhaps they were high school sweethearts, reunited after many years. I had to find out what made them so different.

"'Hi. My name is Stanley Bennett,' I said. 'I've been watching you off and on through dinner. You two are really happy, aren't you? Just out of curiosity, are you folks on your honeymoon like we are? Are you newlyweds?'

"The gray-haired man threw back his head and laughed. 'Newlyweds? Why, son, we've been married fifty-two years! Fifty-two years of love. Fifty-two years of talking across the table. And, you know what? I'm still finding out interesting things about this lovely lady.'"

Uncle Stanley made a decision that night that he's never violated. He decided never to say, "I've learned everything there is to know about my wife." He decided never to say, "I know her like the back of my hand."

He decided never to say it because it's never true. You never can know everything there is to know about another person. We are too wonderfully made to be known completely. We have thoughts, feelings, and memories so rich and complex that a lifetime is not nearly long enough to share them all. More importantly, Stanley decided never to say he knew his wife like the back of his hand because he realized such a statement could kill his marriage. He saw the difference that night between the couples who thought they had nothing to talk about and the one couple who knew they had only just begun.

So Uncle Stanley sat next to Anne and me on the couch the day before our wedding, looked us in the eyes, and said plainly, "Don't ever say that you know everything about one another. Don't ever say, 'I know her like the back my hand.' If you say that, you'll become like one of those couples in the restaurant who stare at their food and look around the room without talking. Instead, expect to discover something new about one another every day."

He continued to explain. "Alan, how old are you? Twenty-three? Okay. Anne, that's twenty-three years he's lived without you. It'll take at least twenty-three years to learn all about his life so far."

He turned to Anne. "Anne, how old are you? Twenty-two? Fine. Alan, that's twenty-two years of life you know nothing about. It'll take at least twenty-two years to discover all the memories she has. Let's see," he figured, "that's forty-five years between the two of you. That's a good start for a marriage. But, hey, by the time you've learned about the first twenty-two years, you'll have lived another twenty-two years. You'll never be able to learn everything there is to learn about your beloved."

When Stanley finished talking, Anne and I agreed we would never say, "I know you like the back of my hand." In our twelve short years of marriage, I've been amazed not at how well I know her but at how little I actually know of her wonderful, complex personality. I discover something new about her every day. It's fascinating.

For example, just yesterday I learned some new things.

I saw a rock Anne painted when she was a girl in elementary school. Her mom has kept it all these years. Now Anne has given it to our little boy, Bennett. It has a glop of yellow paint at the top for a sun and some green splashes toward the bottom to represent grass. In the center stands a plain, red cross. Bennett calls it a smooth stone for knocking down Goliath. I don't know why Anne painted it. I think I'll go ask her. (See? I know so little.)

I watched Anne tune the TV to an old movie we had seen years ago. I discovered that, amazingly, she was able to jump right in. She remembered the exact setting of the scene, the characters' names, and the details of the plot. I was amazed. I, personally, couldn't remember anything about the old movie. How did she remember all that? Hey, I'd better go ask her. See how little I know about her?

We went out to a seafood restaurant last night. Anne ordered broiled shrimp with crabmeat dressing. I'd always thought she hated crabmeat and that she wasn't particularly fond of any form of dressing. Boy, was I wrong. She kept saying, "Wow, this dressing is great." She shared some of the shrimp with me, but I had to beg for a little taste of the crabmeat dressing. I wonder if she'd ever had crabmeat dressing before. Hey, I'll go ask her. You'd think I hardly know my wife at all, wouldn't you?

Anne was in third grade when she painted the rock. She thinks she painted it in Sunday school. She says she always remembers old movies. ("Don't you?" she asked me.) And, no, she'd never had crabmeat dressing before. "Sometimes you just have to branch out," she said. See, I've already learned three new things about her today.

Christians relate to God like most married couples in a restaurant. Too many hardly say a word. Most act like they don't expect anything new to happen.

Your life with God is a marriage. He's chosen you as His bride; you've accepted Him as your Husband. As you dine with Him, you can remain on the edge of your seat and drink in His every word. Or you can skip past familiar Scripture passages, yawning in boredom, looking everywhere except at Him.

You can get lost in prayer, pouring out your heart and listening to His whisper in return. Or you can pray perfunctory pillow-time prayers and fall asleep.

You can tremble in awe as you enter the holy of holies in your worship. Or you can silently say to yourself, *Not this hymn again.*

No one would dare say it with their lips, but plenty of people live as though they believe they know God like the back of their hands. The Christian life is thrilling precisely because we know so little about our heavenly Husband. "As the heavens are higher than the earth, so are my ways higher than your ways and my thoughts than your thoughts" (Isaiah 55:9).

Life with God should never be boring. Our Creator loves to do new things. In the beginning, only God existed. When He spoke to form the world, it was totally and completely new. Seeing that it was good, He kept making new things. Every plant, every flower, every rock, every tree, every animal, Adam, and Eve—God took delight in each one of them.

God wants us to delight in His newness. "Forget the former things; do not dwell on the past. See, I am doing a new thing! Now it springs up; do you not perceive it?" (Isaiah 43:18–19). There is always something wonderful and new to discover about our Lord.

He designed our souls to need fresh grace every day. "His compassions never fail. They are new every morning" (Lamentations 3:22–23).

Remember the manna in the wilderness? Notice the instructions the Lord gave Moses about gathering manna: "Each one is to gather as much as he needs.... No one is to keep any of it until morning." Of course, some "paid no attention to Moses; they kept part of it until morning, but it was full of maggots and began to smell" (Exodus 16:16, 19–20). God's manna must be fresh every morning.

You can't hoard the Bread of Life. Don't forget the Lord's prayer: "Give us this day our daily bread" (Matthew 6:11, KJV, emphasis mine). You can't stockpile the mercy of God.

God wants you to hunger after Him daily. He wants you to lean forward across the candlelit dinner table and hang on His every word. He wants you to ask things of Him and share your heart's hurts with Him. He wants you to thirst for new knowledge of Him. He wants you to learn something new about Him every day.

Try this. The next time you pray, or study the Scriptures, or worship, imagine yourself in a restaurant. Your Spouse sits across the table from you. His name is Jesus. What would you feel? How would you act? I doubt you'd stare at your plate and look passively around the room. The Messiah is sitting across from you. There are unsearchable riches in Him. He lived an eternity before you ever met Him.

I'd better leave you alone now. You have a lot to learn about your Husband.

CHAPTER TWENTY-ONE

FINDING YOUR FIRST LOVE

"Repent and do the things you did at first."
Revelation 2:5

*W*as there ever a time in which you loved God more than you do now? Do you long to fall in love with Jesus all over again?

If so, God's Word has some clear instructions for you. They are the same instructions Jesus gave to the church in Ephesus: "Yet I hold this against you: You have forsaken your first love. Remember the height from which you have fallen! Repent and do the things you did at first" (Revelation 2:4–5).

Three simple steps: Remember. Repent. Relive.

My parishioner Jeff is a good doctor, a good friend, and depending on the day, a good tennis player. But when I learned about the weekend he spent with his wife, I learned he's best at being a husband. Let me step aside while Jeff's wife, Mary, tells it in her own words.

"I just had the nicest surprise of my married life. Last Friday we were winding up our often fast-paced morning routine. After sending the last boy out to the bus, Jeff was on his way out when he took me in his arms and said, 'This is probably not the best time to tell you, but I need to tell you so that you can get ready. We are going on a trip tomorrow. The weather is about the same as it is here, and we'll be doing some walking. There is a special event we will be going to, but you won't need to dress up.'

"He gave me a big hug, and I was smiling with tears in my eyes. I could hardly believe it. It sounded so wonderful, whatever it was. I made a few guesses but was wrong on all counts.

"As we walked down the terminal to the gates, I knew we were on our way to Nashville. I tried to figure out what the event was. I guessed a school reunion or a Christian conference. Then I thought about Nashville being the place where we met—at Vanderbilt—and I asked, 'Does it have anything to do with Nashville being the place where we met? Let's see, twenty years ago...' Jeff quickly changed the subject because he didn't want to give it away right then. I got a lump in my throat to think that this might be a sentimental trip, so I couldn't talk anymore anyway. Jeff said he had been planning this for about eight months.

"After getting settled in our room at a nice, new hotel with lots of marble and people to wait on you hand and foot, we decided to dine at the place where we most often ate during our years in Nashville—Dalt's. They had the best french fries in town. They put some kind of seasoning salt on them that made them great. But the french fries weren't as good as they used to be. I guess after twenty years something had to be different.

"'There is one event that we have to do tonight,' said Jeff. 'We will be walking through the campus.' As we wandered around our college campus, delighting in the beauty and the familiar places, my thoughts drifted to one particular place that held special meaning for both of us. We were headed in that direction. It was the math building.

"Around the top of the math building, five stories up, was a balcony where Jeff had proposed to me on May 11, 1979. It was usually locked up tight, but we had been fortunate many years ago that it was occasionally open. The balcony of an academic building may not sound romantic, but this was no ordinary view. The Vanderbilt campus is incredibly beautiful. All you see are brick pathways through large expanses of green grass accented by huge, old trees. Academic buildings, full of character, dot the landscape, and at night lampposts throw light on the pathways. The steeple of the divinity school is in the background. It's close enough to the tower of Kirkland Hall that you can hear the bells chime. Suffice it to say, it's a very romantic place—a perfect place for a proposal.

"I really didn't think we would be able to get up there. I was hoping, but I didn't hope too hard because I knew it probably would be locked. Jeff was being very casual about our walk. I couldn't tell whether he was thinking about the math building as I was. As we strolled around the computer building, we arrived at the math building.

"The door was open, so we went inside the lobby. A glass box on the wall displayed a list of the current faculty. Jeff leaned against the wall and examined the list. 'I wonder who's still here,' he said.

"I was thinking how great it would be if we could just get onto that balcony. I didn't know if Jeff was thinking the same thing. He was just aimlessly wandering around the lobby. I couldn't stand it. 'Wouldn't it be great,' I said, 'if we could somehow get up to the balcony?'

"'Do you think we could?' Jeff replied offhandedly. Probably not, we both agreed, but we thought we would at least take the elevator to the fifth floor and try the doors.

*W*hen we arrived at the fifth-floor hallway, it was very quiet, and all the offices were locked tight. Papers were plastered on message boards all down the hallway. There were two doors to the balcony, one at each end. We tried one. Locked tight. Then we made the long walk down to the other end. We jiggled it, but it was locked too. My heart sank. We were so close, yet so far. As we were bemoaning the fact that there was no way, I threw out a crazy suggestion. Hoping against hope, I said, 'Why don't you just *try* one of your keys, and see if there's any way it might open the door?'

"As soon as I said it, I knew it was impossible, but I was grasping at straws. Jeff said, 'Okay, I'll try it.' The key slid right into the lock. He turned it, and the lock clicked open. My eyes grew as big as saucers.

"'Wow, I can't believe it!' I said.

"Jeff looked at me with an endearing look and said, 'Now, Mary, you don't think that just *any* key would unlock that door, do you?' He held up the key in his hand, and it was a single key with an unfamiliar key chain. I realized that he had somehow gotten the key…and it all came crashing in: the lengths my husband had gone to in order to recapture one of the most special moments in our lives.

*J*eff told me he had written to the secretary of the math department several months ago to let her in on his secret plan. She agreed and said she would leave a key on top of the faculty roster in the glass box on the wall of the lobby. When Jeff leaned against the wall to look at the list of faculty, he put his hand on top of that box and got the key without my knowing it.

"The view from the balcony was every bit as beautiful as it had been back in our college days. It was peaceful, just as when he proposed. Jeff held me in his arms, and at first all I could do was put my head on his shoulder and cry. I was so overcome by his love for me.

"We reminisced about the time we met, about the romance that led to our marriage. We remembered the time we said good-bye for the summer, knowing we would be apart for at least two years and not knowing whether our relationship would last. I sang to Jeff the song I wrote for him back then.

"We tried to remember the actual way Jeff proposed. We marveled at all the things that had happened in our lives since that time. Before leaving, we bowed our heads, thanked God for His infinite goodness, and prayed for many more good years together.

"The next morning we decided to wander around campus again, visiting as many of our old familiar places as we could. We visited Kissam Quadrangle, where Jeff had roomed his freshman year. We went to the study lounge and marveled that the baseball mitt chair was still there. We ate lunch at the Overcup Oak, the student eatery. We went to a program being sung by the Vanderbilt choir. We went to the dorms we were living in when we first met. We took a picture of Lewis Hall, where I had lived. We remembered how Jeff would appear at my door saying that he was 'just passing by' and thought he would stop to say hi. 'Just passing by'—on the third floor!

"On our last day we knew we just had to go to the Pancake

Pantry where, on many a Saturday morning, we would eat pecan waffles, drink coffee, and talk. We browsed in Village Jewelers, the place where Jeff bought the first expensive gift he ever gave me: a gold cross.

"Our nostalgic weekend had finally come to an end. Here we were, twenty years later, and we had revisited all the old places, meeting students who weren't even born when we met. As we ended this wonderful weekend I remembered the scripture spoken at our wedding: 'Love is as strong as death.... It burns like blazing fire, like a mighty flame. Many waters cannot quench love; rivers cannot wash it away' (Song of Songs 8:6–7).

"In one weekend, my husband gave me enough to fan the flame of our love for another twenty years."

As Jeff did for Mary, so you can fan the flame of your love for God. Jesus instructs, "Yet I hold this against you: You have forsaken your first love. Remember the height from which you have fallen! Repent and do the things you did at first" (Revelation 2:4–5). Remember. Repent. Relive.

Remember the height from which you have fallen.

Christians are prone to spiritual amnesia. We forget the marvels of His love. Remember what it was like to be in love with Him. Remember His first embrace. Remember the miracles. Remember the circumstances in which you met Him. Remember how He proposed salvation to you. Was it through a good friend's witness or an anointed preacher's message? Consider how amazing grace still is. Recall what it was like to move from darkness to light. Remember the time in which your zeal for heaven burned brightly. Drink in the memory. There's power in remembering.

Repent.

To repent means to turn. It is more than a decision. It's a commitment followed by concrete action. It's inserting the key and turning it to open the door. What specific commitment can you make right now? It may be as simple as throwing away the tempting pound cake. It may be as deep as writing a note of confession to the object of your grudge. But repentance means genuine change. It's not just thinking about apologizing; it's picking up the phone. It's not just buying an exercise bike; it's putting your feet on the pedals and pushing.

Relive.

"Do the things you did at first." Did you used to pray, but now you're too busy? Did it feel good when you used to dance for joy in your living room, but now it seems silly? Did you used to have a prayer partner, but now you don't want to be so vulnerable? Try doing the things you did when you first fell in love with God. Don't wait until you "feel like" doing the things you used to do. Just start. Sometimes you have to live yourself into a new way of feeling rather than feel your way into a new way of living.

*I*f you've lost your first love, Jesus is ready to take you back to where your new life began—the foot of the cross. He's ready to take the hidden key and open the door of your heart to the splendors of grace again. He's ready to propose to you once more. Maybe you just need to put your head on His shoulder, hug Him close again, and cry for all He's done for you. Or, better yet, maybe you have a song to sing to Him.

Remember. Repent. Relive. "Many waters cannot quench love; rivers cannot wash it away."

CHAPTER TWENTY-TWO

WALKING IN HIS LOVE

Walk humbly with your God.
Micah 6:8

I don't know why it caught my eye. It was such a little thing. The sermon had been preached. The service was over. No dramatic altar call had been given. No visible angelic visitation. No apparent signs and wonders.

No one noticed. Except the wife, God...and me.

I made my way across the vestibule toward my study to file away the day's sermon. The message preached was a simple one: "Husbands, love your wives as Christ loved the church."

Wonder if it touched anybody? I mused as I tucked away the text and tidied up my desk. I gazed through the office Palladian window into the bright fall afternoon to watch parishioners walk to their cars. As I did so often, I quietly prayed, "Bless this flock, Lord. Every lamb." And that day I added, "Teach these husbands to love their wives as You love us."

That's when I saw it.

A visiting couple walked toward their car. I couldn't have called their names. Other than remembering that they had mentioned grandchildren, I couldn't have told you much of their story. But what I saw made this preacher's heart rejoice.

He took her hand.

It was such a simple sight. Why did it bless me so? Was it the manner in which he took it—so gently, so lovingly? Or was it was my silent wondering, *How long has it been since he took her hand in his?* Or was it the way he walked with her—so proudly, so unhurriedly?

No, it was the simple act's underlying message that touched my heart. That husband's gesture proclaimed Paul's epistle more profoundly than any preacher's most eloquent sermon ever could. "Husbands, love your wives as Christ loved the church."

Those clasped hands defied the world's priorities. The world declares: "Keep your options open." The clasped hands rebutted, "This is my only beloved. I'm a one-woman-kind-of-man, and I like it that way."

It's one thing for an infatuated teenager to hold hands with her latest steady in the high school hallway. But this was a grandfather still clasping the same lady's hand after all those years. I wondered what heartaches had been endured to make that hand clasp still work. I wondered if some desert time had ever threatened to dry up their relationship. I wondered if he'd been a traveling businessman, separated from her for days at a time or perhaps in the service overseas for months on end. I wondered if they still had little nonverbal signals like a gentle hand squeeze to say, "I'm glad you're mine."

It blessed me to consider that their interlocked fingers merely pointed to a far deeper unity. Something of their souls had become interwoven through the warp and woof of married life. Clasped hands gave proof of cleaving hearts.

The husband was a sizable man. Not obese, but strong. I felt sure he was a leader. He took her hand, and she received his hand's embrace in return. He seemed to direct their steps as he guided her to the passenger side of the car. He opened the door, and once she was secure, he made his way to the driver's seat.

It's beautiful to consider his leadership. He took the initiative—with her hand, with the path, with the door. He took the lead confidently and proudly. But he did not outpace her and drag her from his backside. Nor did he lag behind her to push or prod her onward. He walked proudly by her side.

Maybe that's what blessed me most. When a husband holds his wife's hand, he doesn't walk in front of her or behind her. He walks beside her.

I stood at the window, suspended in time, as though I had just seen God. I was blessed by the simple profundity of the husband's unnoticed act. I was blessed to think that something of the gospel had gone into him that day. "Husbands, love your wives as Christ loved the church."

Then a startling, deeper, blessed awareness settled upon my soul. What I had beheld was not just a scene of how a husband loves his wife. I had seen a picture of how Christ loves His bride.

The Lord didn't wait for me to reach for His hand. Instead, He stepped down from heaven and stretched His hand toward me. It happened so quietly, so unobtrusively. Amid a busy Bethlehem, hardly anyone noticed that God had come to earth. Only some angels, a few shepherds, and some observant scholars saw it. The Groom had come to take His bride by the hand.

After all the years of the bride's rebellion and even her harlotry, He still came to put His hand in hers. That first

Christmas, God reminded the whole watching cosmos, *Nothing can separate Me from My beloved.*

Think of it. After all the desert days of your doubts and disobedience, Jesus still wants to take your hand. He wants to interweave His life into yours. With a gentle squeeze He reminds you that His love has not diminished. As His fingers interlock with yours, He testifies to all the powers and principalities of the unseen world that His hand clasp still works.

More wonderfully, consider this: Your heavenly Husband is the King of kings. All things are subject to His sovereign rule. And He indeed rules. Whatever He says goes. You are the disciple, He is the teacher. You are the creature, He is the Creator. You are of dust, He is of eternity. You are soiled, He is spotless. You are the follower, He is the leader.

Yet He invites you to walk by His side.

The Bible repeatedly calls our life a "walk." "We walk by faith, not by sight" (2 Corinthians 5:7, KJV). God walked with Adam and Eve in the garden (Genesis 3:8). Godly men like Noah are heralded as ones who "walked with God" (Genesis 6:9). The law of Moses repeatedly commands us: "Walk in all the way that the LORD your God has commanded you" (Deuteronomy 5:33).

I had always pictured the Christian life as a walk toward God, a walk behind God, and a walk in the manner of God. But as I watched the grandfather clasp his wife's hand and walk her to the car after church that day, it occurred to me: The heavenly Husband wants to walk with His bride.

Micah 6:8 is well known: "He has showed you, O man, what is good. And what does the LORD require of you? To act justly and to love mercy and to walk humbly with your God." The words raise our gaze to the pinnacle of prophetic exhortation. The prophet saw the heart of God and announced what pleases the Lord most. God is not interested in burnt offerings; He's interested in humbled hearts.

What a verse! The greatest, noblest virtues are there—justice, mercy, humility. But you've probably never noticed the most surprising word in the verse: "with." It's a Hebrew preposition, and it really means "with." *The Theological Wordbook of the Old Testament* provides these possible definitions: "with," "beside," "by," "among," "accompanying," "from among," or "between." It never means "behind" or "before." To quote the scholars, "The preposition…expresses the concept of inclusiveness, together-ness, company."[1]

Imagine that. God wants to walk *with* you. Yes, He wants your obedience, your service, and your faith. But above all, He wants your company.

I love walking with my wife. Where do we walk? Nowhere in particular. We take strolls around the neighborhood. We take long walks at the beach. It doesn't really matter where we are headed—as long as I'm with her. The togetherness is more important than the destination. It doesn't matter so much which turns we take, as long as we're walking hand in hand. It doesn't matter what sights we see, as long as I get to escort her back into our home when the walk is done.

*G*od's greatest desire is to walk with you—hand in hand. Of course He wants your allegiance. Sure, it's important that you walk the path of righteousness and cultivate your capacity to walk by faith. But I'm now convinced, the destination of life's journey doesn't matter nearly as much as your togetherness with God along life's paths. The bumps and turns and sights along the road don't matter that much as long as the Husband is still at your side at the end, escorting you home.

Be still, bride of Christ. Your heavenly Husband's hand awaits your clasp. It is a strong hand—strong enough to pull you from the deepest pit. It is a gentle hand—deft enough to count your hairs, your freckles, and your teardrops. It is a well-worn hand—callused from hard work, splintered from carrying a cross, scarred from the pierce of nails.

It is a holy hand that tolerates no evil, but it's not a clenched fist. It is a captivating clasp, but it's no angry prison-guard's grip. It is a joyful hand, but it's more than the high-five of a teammate. It is a hand of promise, but it transcends the firm handshake of a business partner.

It is the hand of a Husband in love.

Invisible fingers interlock with yours to show how closely He wants His own Spirit interwoven with yours. With gentleness and strength, His invisible clasp tells your soul of His desire to cleave unto you. He hasn't run in front of you waiting for you to catch up with Him. He hasn't pushed you out front to carve paths He's yet to travel. Instead, this heavenly Husband leads while at your side. He holds your hand because He wants to walk *with* you.

I never had a chance to tell the visitor how I silently observed his quiet act of affection toward his wife that day. But I won't forget it. Who can describe the feeling a woman has when her husband still wants to hold her hand? Who can describe the ache of a woman whose husband does not? It was such a little thing, such a simple gesture. But heaven was in his clasp. So I want to say, "Wherever you are, sir, thanks for taking her hand."

And I must turn my moist eyes heavenward to declare, "Thank You, Lord, for not leaving my fingers empty. There's no place my hand would rather be than in Yours. I don't care where we're going as long as I'm walking in Your love."

CHAPTER TWENTY-THREE

LOOSE-DIRT LONGINGS

As long as we are at home in the body
we are away from the Lord.
2 Corinthians 5:6

ad Bernice lived a few months more, she and Claude would have celebrated their sixtieth wedding anniversary.

Sixty years. How do sixty anniversaries shape two souls? I've been married twelve—a pittance by comparison. After my brief twelve years of marriage,

> ...there is an empty echo in the house if Anne is gone for more than a day, a hollowness in my heart if she's gone more than two.
>
> ...I haven't just accommodated to her tastes in restaurants, vacation spots, and home decor; my desires actually have become like her longings.
>
> ...I realize that I shift no life-gear, make no decision, and seal no commitment without somehow asking, "Will this bless my beloved?"

If my life has been shaped so deeply after a short twelve years, what happens to a man's character after five times my married life? That's the question that quietly captivated my mind as I watched Claude make his last pause at his wife's fresh grave before he was escorted back to the funeral car. What does a man feel when he stands in the loose dirt that lies by the casket of his bride of sixty years?

An embrace and a prayer were all I could give. I dared not offer other words as if to pretend I knew his pain. I would never boast to say I understood his anguish. But I think I heard his thoughts. Allow me a moment to explain. I think you'll hear them too.

"Bernice was a miracle," everyone told me. Cancer had thinned her to nearly nothing and drained her down to death's door years before. Some just said she had spunk and a fighting spirit. Believers knew the Lord had healed her. No matter what people believed, I'm sure glad she lived those seven extra years. Those were the years I was privileged to be her pastor. I took bus trips to view North Carolina's fall foliage with her and the other church seniors who refused to let grass grow under their feet. I got to sample the way she prepared the vegetables Claude grew in his garden. I got to hear her tell stories of the church's early days. And I watched her love her husband.

"I can't do a thing with him," she would say of her eighty-seven-year-old husband who still plowed his garden with a mule. What she meant was, "Isn't Claude remarkable? What other man is there like him?"

"I can't do a thing with him" meant "What would I do without him?" Simply put, Bernice loved Claude and Claude adored Bernice.

*W*hen the cancer came back, Bernice declined quickly. She never went to the hospital, never resided in the nursing home. At the end she was confined to her own bed. One night as Bernice was drifting into unconsciousness, Claude decided to sleep beside her once again. He crawled into the bed, pulled the covers up, and took one last look at his beloved. In the middle of the night, their watching daughter spoke. "Daddy."

Claude woke up in the bed. Bernice woke up in heaven.

It could have happened in reverse order. After all, Claude was older. Eighty-seven. That's partly why I think I heard Claude's thoughts as he stood in the loose dirt next to the grave. He was so close to heaven himself. Didn't he ask himself, *Why am I still here?* Didn't he wonder, *How will I live without her?* And as his eyes looked heavenward, didn't he quietly hope, *Lord, let me join her soon?*

An eighty-seven-year-old man who loses a wife of sixty years doesn't think about new hobbies or new wives. He thinks about heaven's reunion. The world becomes strangely unappetizing. The hunger for heaven intensifies. And as so often happens, the bereaved soon leaves the earth too.

What's Claude doing now? I can't say for sure. I live in a different town and pastor a different church now. But I guess Claude does the things he's always done. He works his garden. He pulls some weeds. He plants some seeds. He plucks some ripened vegetables. He carries the corn and beans into the kitchen.

But the kitchen is quiet. There's no Bernice at the sink to say, "Claude, what am I going to do with all these vegetables?" There's no grinning face or clanking pots. So Claude is at home—and yet he's like a stranger in his own kitchen. Maybe the thought darts again through his mind: *Lord, let me see her soon.*

*T*o understand Claude's loose-dirt longings, come with me to observe another widower standing beside his aged wife's grave. Like Claude, this man had kept the same bride for more years than I've been alive. Like Claude, he loved his wife like his own soul. And, like Claude, he must have had some heavenward longings.

His name was Abraham. His grief is recorded in Genesis 23.

"Sarah lived to be a hundred and twenty-seven years old. She died...in the land of Canaan, and Abraham went to mourn for Sarah and to weep over her" (Genesis 23:1–2).

Sarah was 65 when she left Haran with her husband to follow him into the ministry. She was 127 years old when she died. That's 62 years Abraham and Sarah had walked with each other as they walked with God. They experienced the triumphs and tragedies of life together. They had tasted the bitter pang of hope deferred as they held the promise of offspring but held no baby. They laughed separately, but loudly, when the Lord assured her at ninety that she would soon give birth. Perhaps they cried together when little Isaac was born. Abraham named the boy, but I bet Sarah suggested the Hebrew name meaning "he laughs." They faced tough parenting issues and underwent times of testing. In peaceful times, perhaps they spent long evenings just counting stars and thanking God for their growing family.

Be sure of this. Abraham loved his wife deeply. When Sarah

went into the grave, Abraham stood in the loose dirt and wept.

Do you wonder what he was thinking? Ponder the odd conversation that followed.

"Then Abraham rose from beside his dead wife and spoke to the Hittites. He said, 'I am an alien and a stranger among you. Sell me some property for a burial site here so I can bury my dead'" (Genesis 23:3–4).

"The Hittites replied to Abraham, 'Sir, listen to us. You are a mighty prince among us. Bury your dead in the choicest of our tombs'" (23:5–6).

How strange. Abraham called himself "an alien and a stranger." The Hittites called him "a mighty prince."

Perhaps Abraham was simply demonstrating his clever bartering skills. Verses 7–16 sound like a Middle-Eastern merchant haggling with a tourist over the price of an olive-wood nativity scene.

Nonetheless, don't miss the irony. Abraham was burying his wife in the promised land, but he knew he wasn't home yet.

"An alien and a stranger" or "a mighty prince." Which was the patriarch?

He was both.

He was the bearer of the promise of God—an heir of God's blessing. *And* he was a pilgrim, just passing through. "By faith [Abraham] made his home in the promised land like a stranger in a foreign country; he lived in tents, as did Isaac and Jacob, who were heirs with him of the same promise. For he was looking forward to the city with foundations, whose architect and builder is God" (Hebrews 11:9–10).

Abraham was both alien *and* ruler, stranger *and* prince.

So is every child of God.

You are more than a conqueror in Christ, heir of royal riches. But you are also an alien in the world. You're a prince or princess. But you're also a stranger here. No matter how good it gets, it'll never be quite good enough on earth. No matter how good your bed feels, you're never in your real home until your head's on a heavenly pillow.

You are a bride whose Bridegroom awaits you in eternity.

You have His Spirit. You get delicious tastes of joy and peace. But you know there is going to be more. Your recurring hunger proves it.

When you've been with your mate long enough, you can hardly bear being separated. When you've been separated long enough, you'd just about give up your earthly life to be back together.

How else can you understand a man like Paul who says: "For to me, to live is Christ and to die is gain. If I am to go on living in the body, this will mean fruitful labor for me. Yet what shall I choose? I do not know! I am torn between the two: I desire to depart and be with Christ, which is better by far; but it is more necessary for you that I remain in the body" (Philippians 1:21–24).

Paul sounds like a man who misses his mate. He explained his feelings to the Corinthians: "Now we know that if the earthly tent we live in is destroyed, we have a building from God, an eternal house in heaven, not built by human hands. Meanwhile we groan, longing to be clothed with our heavenly dwelling.... Now it is God who has made us for this very purpose and has given us the Spirit as a deposit, guaranteeing what is to come. Therefore we are always confident and know that as long as we are at home in the body we are away from the Lord" (2 Corinthians 5:1–2, 5–6).

*T*dare not say I knew how Claude felt. Bernice had been by his side for sixty years. What does a husband feel when he wakes up in a bed next to a wife who doesn't wake up? I've never felt what my saintly, aged friend felt. But can't you hear his thoughts now? *Lord, let me see her soon.*

It only makes sense. When you've linked your souls and latched your hands for such a long season, you can hardly tolerate the distance.

I say it at times. "Lord, my heavenly Bridegroom, come soon." I love my wife, I cherish my little boy. I'm thrilled when preaching, writing, or praying. I have fun on the golf course. Life is sometimes delectable. But it's not enough. There must be more. So I'm sure glad this isn't all there is. I want to see Him face to face.

Don't you too? Even people who doubt He's there long to see Him. Even if you are still too much a friend of the world, you miss Him. That ache in your heart that just doesn't go away? That gnawing dissatisfaction with the glitter of possessions? That odd loneliness you feel even in the midst of a crowd? They're loose-dirt longings. It's only natural for the bride to want to be with her Bridegroom.

Sure, you're a child of the King. But you're also an alien. When you long for a better day, wait and weep. Trust and pray. But don't despair. He wants to see your face in heaven even more than you want to see His. Loose-dirt longings will not linger forever. Claude will see Bernice. If you're the bride of Christ, one day you'll see the Lover of your soul face to face.

CHAPTER TWENTY-FOUR

A HUSBAND'S GOOD NIGHT

...prepared as a bride beautifully dressed for her husband.
Revelation 21:2

*G*ood night, my sleeping beauty. I enjoyed our evening together.

Life is so full for us now—a busy church to pastor, a busy boy to parent. Good things. Fruitful, productive things. But busy things.

But tonight we had no toddler's chicken nuggets to chop up, did we? Just your veal forester and my steak *au poivre*. Tonight we solved no church crises, made no ministry plans. Such unproductive time—a dinner and a ballet. Ah, to waste more such evenings with you.

Remember the night we first talked—how we conversed until the dawn? I remember running straight to my early class, alive and full of wonder. Sounds so tiring now. So foolish. So impractical.

Could we do it again sometime? Stay up all night just talking, giggling, and dreaming.

A lifetime of all-night conversations could never quench my thirst to know you.

Did I mention how beautiful you looked tonight? The sequins on your black dress really sparkled—the way your eyes always do.

And, by the way, thanks for snickering at my silly jokes tonight. Nothing makes my heart more glad than seeing joy in you.

Except, perhaps, this soft peace that has settled on your sleeping face.

I double-checked the doors the way you like me to. They're locked tight. Sleep safely, darling. But don't you know, I'd fling my frame in the path of any crook who creaked the door toward you. If the moment ever came, I'd want to be your hero.

Sleep well, no need ever to fret. If you ever need some cheering, I'll be your favorite fan. And if you ever need bread for the baking, I'll find a way to win it.

The walk back to the free parking lot from the auditorium was chilly, wasn't it? I know, I know. I could have parked in the deck. It would have been closer. It wasn't just the three-dollar garage fee that led me down the road. Have you figured it out after all these years of our *Nutcracker* tradition? I like that cold, two-block walk. I like the way you squeeze my hand and snuggle up for warmth while the wind whistles down the street.

I suppose I'd better close my eyes now, love. It seems like there was something bothering me earlier. What was it? Something you said? Some oversight? Let me think. Oh well, I forgive you. I can't remember it anyway. In fact, at the moment, I can't think of anything you've ever done wrong. Sleep well, sweet wife. Sleep well.

With a kiss I seal the bliss of this good night. Never doubt my love, my darling Anne. No matter what, I'll always hold your hand.

Lord, bless my sleeping wife. And Lord, please bless me. For

You know the frailty of this husband's flesh. I want to be her confidant, but You know my hearing slips. I want to be her hero, but You know my knees can knock. I want her walking by my side, but You know my feet can stumble. Oh Lord, if her hand is soft and mine is strong, I'll hold hers through both joy and trouble. But if my strong grip is clasped to hers, who will hold my own weak hand?

I will hold it, dear one. I made your hand for Mine. More than you want her steps beside you, I want you walking by My side.

I know she's your bride, little child, but remember, you are such for Me.

I noticed you the way you noticed her, and I put you in My plan. I sailed past a trillion stars just to stand at the door of your heart to knock. I sent you notes that you didn't know were from Me, and I whispered to you in your sleep.

I gave you a taste of My love so you could see that it was sweet. I allured you with a sunset, and I met you in your pain. I put people in your path who would tell you about my smile.

I wooed you because I wanted your hand. Why would I leave it empty now?

So, sleep well, My chosen partner. I know you are tired. But someday soon we'll again stay up all night long and talk. I know your thoughts, but, oh, what thoughts I have toward you.

Let your heart be light. My joy will be your blanket. My peace will be your pillow.

Fret not, beloved boy and bride, the doors to darkness are all locked. And while you sleep, I'll stay awake and return to you all that has been stolen. Just tell someone in the morning that your Hero is your Husband.

Oh, wait, there was that error. What sin was that? I can't see it for the blood. I forgive you. In fact, at the moment I can't remember anything you've ever done wrong.

Sleep well, My now-unblemished bride. Let Me seal My affection with the kiss of My own Spirit. For as you rest by your beloved, My love will rest on you. As you are groom to her, even more am I to you. Whatever you want for her, I want all the more for you. You can never love her in the measure that I love you. You have her only for her earthly span—and I am your soul's Lover forever. So, sleep well, beloved. Sleep well.

Multnomah Publishers®

The publisher and author would love to hear your comments about this book. *Please contact us at:* www.multnomah.net/loverofmysoul

NOTES

Chapter One: Wooed

1. Cynthia C. Muchnick, *101 Ways to Pop the Question* (New York: Macmillan, 1997), 115–6.

Chapter Two: Pursued

1. Patricia's story appears in Robert Fulghum, *True Love* (New York: HarperCollins, 1997), 66–70.

Chapter Four: The Bride from the Brothel

1. For creative ideas I have borrowed generously from T. D. Jakes's videotape message "The God Who Married a Tramp" and from Francine Rivers's novel *Redeeming Love* (Sisters, Ore.: Multnomah Publishers, 1997).

Chapter Eight: True Hero

1. Dini von Mueffling, *The 50 Most Romantic Things Ever Done* (New York: Doubleday, 1997), 23–4.

Chapter Eleven: Taking His Name

1. Jay Leno, comp., *Jay Leno's Real but Ridiculous Headlines from America's Newspapers* (New York: Wings Books, 1992), 352, 354.
2. As told by Brennan Manning at First Presbyterian Church, Winston-Salem, North Carolina, November 18–20, 1990.

Chapter Thirteen: Sweet Somethings in Your Ear
1. Retold from Max Lucado, *When God Whispers Your Name* (Dallas: Word Publishing, 1994), 167–9.

Chapter Fifteen: When Tripping Keeps You from Falling
1. Fulghum, *True Love,* 42–4.

Chapter Eighteen: My Champion
1. Charlie W. Shedd, *Letters to Karen: On Keeping Love in Marriage* (Nashville: Abingdon Press, 1965), 34–5.

Chapter Twenty-Two: Walking in His Love
1. R. Laird Harris, Gleason L. Archer Jr., and Bruce K. Waltke, eds., *The Theological Wordbook of the Old Testament* (Chicago: Moody Press, 1980), 676.